Praise for *Three Simple Lines* by Natalie Goldberg

"Natalie Goldberg takes haiku, a subject few of us in Western culture richly understand, and unearths the themes of human life we all yearn for and recognize: connection, loss, wandering, arrival. She shows us how to pay great attention to what really matters. This book is the salve our chaotic world needs right now."

— **BILL ADDISON**, food critic, *Los Angeles Times*

"The wide-open, engaged mind and pen of Natalie Goldberg, a pilgrimage to Japan, and haiku — what could be better? *Three Simple Lines* is a sweet and moving read about the mysterious connections, across cultures and time, that exquisite writing can make. As Goldberg walks the trails and visits the graves of Basho, Buson, and others, she brings us home to the shattering feeling of being alive — the feeling of haiku."

— **NORMAN FISCHER**, Zen priest, poet, and author of
Training in Compassion

"This exquisite book takes you into the heart of the mystery of haiku and into Natalie Goldberg's remarkable and intimate discoveries about Japan and herself, by walking in the footsteps of great haiku writers of former times. Laced with threads of sorrow, humor, and wisdom, *Three Simple Lines* will be cherished by all of us for its humanness, bravery, and brilliance."

— **REV. JOAN JIKO HALIFAX**, abbot at Upaya Zen Center

"In *Three Simple Lines*, Natalie Goldberg blends memoir with the lyrical history of a poetic form. The result is an unclassifiable book that is utterly poignant, riveting, and hypnotic. It is a book that, in the truest sense, achieves transcendence."

— **CHIGOZIE OBIOMA**, author of the Booker Prize finalists
The Fishermen and *An Orchestra of Minorities*

"This is a wonderful immersion into haiku and, thankfully, more than three lines."

— **RED PINE / BILL PORTER**, author of
Finding Them Gone: Visiting China's Poets of the Past

"Natalie Goldberg's writing always offers a respite from the world, which it achieves by diving right into the madness of the moment. Like the haiku she reads, writes, and treasures, *Three Simple Lines* is a refuge in a chaotic world. Through her travels in Japan to seek the origins of haiku, she reveals the honest struggle of being a writer and, just beneath that, the honest struggle of being human."
— **JENN SHAPLAND,** author of the National Book Award finalist
My Autobiography of Carson McCullers

"This jewel of a book represents a dream meeting between subject and author. Natalie Goldberg's trademark prose — wonderfully clear, simple, and deep — takes us into her profound understanding of haiku and makes this story of her search for haiku's origins among beautiful gardens, mountains, modern cities, and ancient temples compelling and gripping. It's also the ideal meeting of verse and prose: The haiku are embedded in a limpid narrative, free-flowing and irresistible as a mountain stream. When they appear now and then as beautiful stepping-stones in a journey of discovery, they come alive in ways that still the mind, expand time, and open the heart. A classic narrative of discovery and homage — and a simple, humble book to fall in love with."
— **HENRY SHUKMAN,** author of
One Blade of Grass: Finding the Old Road of the Heart

"Like haiku itself, Natalie Goldberg's *Three Simple Lines* is spare, keenly observed, and blessedly light on its feet. This wise and spirited travelogue acquaints us with some of the form's legendary practitioners — and reminds us just how much of life's magic can be packed into a few inspired words."
— **HAMPTON SIDES,** *New York Times* bestselling author of
Ghost Soldiers and *On Desperate Ground*

Three
Simple
Lines

Also by Natalie Goldberg

MEMOIR

Long Quiet Highway: Waking Up in America
The Great Failure: My Unexpected Path to Truth
Living Color: Painting, Writing, and the Bones of Seeing
Let the Whole Thundering World Come Home

ESSAYS

The Great Spring: Writing, Zen, and This Zigzag Life
The Truth of This Life by Katherine Thanas,
edited by Goldberg and Anelli

POETRY

Chicken and in Love
Top of My Lungs: Poems and Paintings

WRITING BOOKS

Writing Down the Bones: Freeing the Writer Within
Wild Mind: Living the Writer's Life
Thunder and Lightning: Cracking Open the Writer's Craft
Old Friend from Far Away: The Practice of Writing Memoir
The True Secret of Writing: Connecting Life with Language

NOVEL

Banana Rose

NOTEBOOK

Essential Writer's Notebook

DOCUMENTARY FILM

Tangled Up in Bob: Searching for Bob Dylan
(with filmmaker Mary Feidt)

Three Simple Lines

A Writer's Pilgrimage into
the Heart and Homeland of Haiku

Natalie Goldberg

New World Library
Novato, California

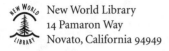

New World Library
14 Pamaron Way
Novato, California 94949

Text design by Tona Pearce Myers

Permissions acknowledgments beginning on page 153 are an extension of the copyright page.

Library of Congress Cataloging-in-Publication Data

Names: Goldberg, Natalie, author.
Title: Three simple lines : a writer's pilgrimage into the heart and homeland of haiku / Natalie Goldberg.
Description: Novato, California : New World Library, [2021] | Includes bibliographical references. | Summary: "An autobiographical meditation on the writing and reading of haiku, the essence of haiku mind, and the country and culture that nurtured the form"-- Provided by publisher.
Identifiers: LCCN 2020039241 (print) | LCCN 2020039242 (ebook) | ISBN 9781608686971 (hardcover) | ISBN 9781608686988 (epub)
Subjects: LCSH: Haiku. | Haiku--History and criticism. | American poetry --Japanese influences.
Classification: LCC PL759 .G65 2021 (print) | LCC PL759 (ebook) | DDC 811/.6--dc23
LC record available at https://lccn.loc.gov/2020039241
LC ebook record available at https://lccn.loc.gov/2020039242

First printing, January 2021
ISBN 978-1-60868-697-1
Ebook ISBN 978-1-60868-698-8
Printed in the USA on 30% postconsumer-waste recycled paper

New World Library is proud to be a Gold Certified Environmentally Responsible Publisher. Publisher certification awarded by Green Press Initiative.

10   9   8   7   6   5   4   3   2

For Upaya Zen Center,
where haiku blooms every February

And for Roshi Joan Halifax,
Upaya's founding teacher
and my good friend

Follow your inner moonlight.
Don't hide the madness.
            ALLEN GINSBERG

Contents

Nothing Less Than God

Haiku is a refuge when the world seems chaotic, when you are lost, frightened, tangled, and nothing is clear.

> Unaware
> the place is famous
> a man tilling a field
> SHIKI

I read this and cock my head, listening deeper than my pain and confusion — a prominent place, a man doing what's in front of him.

I read another:

> Peeling a pear —
> a trickle of sweet juice
> along the blade
> SHIKI

I smile. I've seen that on the knife many times, and now Shiki has made me conscious of it. Something sexy about it too.

1

A flea-bite also;
when she is young,
is beautiful
ISSA

Is it the actual bite, round and pink, that is beautiful? Or
the young girl who got it? Or is there no difference? An insect
bite is elemental. My busy thoughts are settling. My curiosity
is piqued. The complicated world is made of simple elements.

The evening cool,
knowing the bell
is tolling our life away
ISSA

That bell that strikes at twilight marks another day passing.
All these years I heard the big hollow sound in the zendo or in
a distant church, and an unnamable emotion rose in me, but I
never articulated what it was. Of course, *impermanence*. Maybe
I didn't want to know. One full turn of the sun after another.
Nothing to grab on to. I move deeper into the truth of my life.

Dear, dear,
what a fat, happy face it has,
this peony!
ISSA

The first time I saw a peony was with Jim White, a fine
poet. We were walking down Emerson Avenue in Minneapolis
in the springtime, and there they were, big, almost rotund,

the buds enormous. "You know how they open?" Jim said, bending down with his big body. "They secrete a sweet sap that attracts the ants; the ants crawl in and open the petals." He bent closer and touched one, named it: "Peony."

A whole universe of the Midwest opened. Later I found peonies, petunias, and zinnias in other places, but for me they originated in the heart of the country.

Now haiku has woken up memory, led me to grief. Jim died too young of an enlarged heart.

> The piercing cold —
> in our bedroom stepping
> on my dead wife's comb
> BUSON

I am sailing far beyond the original agony that drove me to haiku an hour ago.

That's okay.

Any emotion one feels, pure and simple, moves, passes, if accepted. Earlier I was trying to dominate my confusion, make it clear. Haiku reminds me that it clears on its own, with patience, over time.

Allen Ginsberg, the poet, first introduced me to haiku. "There are four great Japanese haiku writers," he declared, holding up a finger for each one as he named them, in front of the class in summer 1976. We were at Naropa Institute in Boulder, Colorado. "Basho, Buson, Issa, and Shiki."

No women? I thought. Okay, I'd take the boys on and learn what I could from them, sure there were some women hidden in history.

He also told us that the formal five syllables, then seven, then five, often taught in Western schools, does not necessarily work in English. In Japanese each syllable counts. They don't have *the, an, that,* those articles of speech, so he encouraged us not to worry about the count if we write or translate haiku. Only make sure the three lines make the mind leap.

"The only real measure of a haiku," Allen told us that one hot July afternoon, "is upon hearing one, your mind experiences a small sensation of space" — he paused; I leaned in, breathless — "which is nothing less than God."

Now, in 2012, on the cusp of age sixty-six, I am about to search for a grave near the foothills of Mount Hiei: Buson's. The eighteenth-century painter and haiku master. Of the four named by Ginsberg, I found Buson to be the least accessible in translation. Only one or two books of his work have been translated into English.

Buson, who was born in 1716, after Basho died, was deeply inspired by him. Buson considered Basho his haiku master.

The temple I plan to visit on the outskirts of Kyoto, where Buson is buried, is also famous for Basho's hut, though it is not clear if Basho, with his walking stick, actually stopped at that precise place on his wanderings while he circumambulated

Mount Hiei, "shading the dust from his eyes" — the Zen way of saying "seeing clearly."

But when Buson visited the hut years later, the grass room was only a pile of dirt. Buson engaged friends to rebuild it with him. He was a social man, though he, like Basho, had spent time — five years — practicing in Buddhist temples as a lay priest. But he did not seem to have the desire for purification that drove Basho. Buson had a wife and daughter, and in his sixties, through the success of his paintings, was able to own a house in Kyoto.

After rebuilding Basho's hut, Buson and his friends, as a way to honor Basho's art, all vowed to meet there without fail twice a year to write haiku together and drink sake.

Before Basho, *hokku*, which later became the basis for the independent structure of haiku, was the starting verse of *renga*, a Japanese linked collaborative poetic form of at least two stanzas used for humorous entertainment at parties, to flirt with a courtesan, to display one's cleverness. Basho took that first verse seriously, connected it to life and death, to a spiritual path, piercing through the blinding activities of daily life in the regimented society of seventeenth-century Japan to express the true muscle of a person's being.

What is the Way of haiku? Bare attention, no distractions, pure awareness, noticing only what is in the moment. Being connected to seasons, unconnected to self-clinging. And then, out of that, composing your experience in three lines that go beyond logic, that make the mind leap. In the center, a taste of emptiness. A frog, a crow, a turnip — the ordinary right in front of you is the realm of awakening. Pure Zen but not Zen.

"If you write five haiku in a lifetime, you are a haiku writer. If you write ten, you are a master," Basho said. He didn't mean don't practice, don't try, but he was saying the stakes were high. In writing a real one, the world drops away, mind and body shatter, and the only thing left is the crow cawing. You've dropped the old yellow coat of yourself, your sorrow, desire, indifference — the world has stepped forward and you have stepped back, another way of coming home. To put this experience down in three lines is to transmit a taste of what is possible and pass it on. Great generosity. You penetrate down through the generations.

> Even Basho
> right up to death
> longed for a haiku
> N.G.

> How I long to see
> among the morning flowers
> the face of God
> BASHO

Though Basho and Buson studied in monasteries, they never became monks; they took their lives outside the cloistered walls into the immense world of nature. Both brought their understanding into poems that were passed down, but the haiku poems were not always immediately understandable. I contemplated Basho's most famous one for a long time:

> Frog jumps
> in old pond
> water sound

I've seen different translations — for instance:

> Old pond
> frog jumps in
> plop!

> Ancient pond —
> frog jumps in
> sound of the water

I've also seen this haiku made fun of, maybe because it's simple yet painfully elusive. You know there is something there, but what? I feel the frustration:

> Old poet jumps in
> Frog jumps out

But nonetheless, Basho's haiku is serious and carries some quintessential cultural and aesthetic significance. Everyone in Japan knows it.

Was it morning, as I was munching toast outside? Or turning a corner in the car? Or glancing at my watch, about to go to an appointment? Yes, that was it — reaching for the knob, the door casing, the single window in the green-painted wood, I stepped over the threshold — his mind was empty, that's all there was, sitting or standing by the water — the flash movement of the frog, then the sound, the sound, the sound, filling his ears, his mind and heart. Nothing else in the whole world. The realization poured through me like a waterfall, rushing to the bottom.

It might have been a dentist appointment. Piles of People *magazines, two stray* New Yorkers, *a white paper cup of half-drunk tea on a table, the round impression of another one on the glass surface, hum of a drill in a room beyond the waiting room. I was no longer waiting. I had arrived in the middle of a famous haiku, no longer left out, outside, wanting in. No in or out. No nothing. Something. The old pond of the mind finally quiet.*

Here's another translation:

> At the ancient pond
> a frog plunges into
> the sound of water

Here Basho is that frog.

The Narrow Road to the Deep North by Basho was read by many members of my generation. The "deep north" indicates the darkness, the unknown, the cold and scary. Also, it was the name of an actual road in Honshu, the largest Japanese island.

Austere, driven, serious, not mixing with society, never married, Basho followed this Way of haiku, wandering to distant and wild parts of Japan, carrying spare necessities, sometimes accompanied by a haiku disciple or a lover — maybe one and the same. He was a homosexual — something kept quiet in the annals of history — and sometimes he traveled alone. While he journeyed, he opened himself to the trees, ponds, birds, insects, rural people — first expressed in short prose, then with a leap into haiku, those penetrating three short lines that make time stop. Back and forth — prose, haiku — together called *haibun*.

My connection with Buson happened later than that with Basho. I met Buson in 1993, when I'd gone for the weekend, back when it was funky and cheap, to Ojo Caliente, a hot springs spa in northern New Mexico. We rented a small cottage, replete with pale-yellow linoleum floors, creaky doors, lumpy bed, painted wood knobs on cabinets, and a kitchen with Formica counters, square table, and four matching yellow chairs, all for $48 a night. I even schlepped in a Hibachi for barbecuing steaks on the back porch.

Almost as an afterthought, as I'd darted out my back door for the weekend, I grabbed R.H. Blyth's *Haiku, Volume 1: Eastern Culture*. Ginsberg had said, "Get Blyth if you want a good translation."

Reginald Horace Blyth (1898–1964) was tutor to the crown prince of Japan when the war broke out and was incarcerated for its duration. Not wanting to waste time, he deepened his understanding of the Japanese language and discovered its literature while in the internment camp. He also met Robert Aitken in Japan in 1944. The two men had frequent discussions about Zen.

Aitken had been living in Guam as a civilian, working in construction at the beginning of World War II. He was detained by the Japanese and held in internment camps for the duration of the war. When Aitken returned to the States, he studied English literature and received an MA in Japanese. Eventually becoming a revered Zen teacher in the Unites States, he wrote, among other books, *Zen Waves*, in which each chapter illuminates a single Basho haiku. Decades earlier, when I was a young hippie, that book had shed volumes of light on my twenty-something mind, as I read it atop the thin floor mattress in our old threadbare adobe in the Talpa hills. These were the beginning illuminations, like fireflies from another world, dropped into the crinoline creases of my brain and never forgotten.

When we hit Ojo, I immediately became ensconced in the Blyth haiku book. The first day passed with my nose rarely out of it. This was not the original plan. I was with a new girlfriend. It was supposed to be a romantic getaway. My attention manifested like this: "Hey, listen to this haiku." I read aloud.

The lightly freckled Irish skin around my girlfriend's eyes crinkled; her upper lip showed her small teeth in a half smile. She said nothing. I ignored any signs of discontent.

My new girlfriend, on the second morning of our three-day weekend, realized the only way to get through to me was with haiku. At breakfast over scrambled eggs, cheese, and tortillas she burst out,

> Kiss me, you fool
> Winter is coming

My head jerked up. I grabbed her.

But the next day I was at it again. Soaking in the old hot springs, the sun nakedly glaring down, my hair dripping, a wet towel around my shoulders, I opened the book again. In the bottom left corner, a haiku:

> Ah, grief and sadness!
> The fishing line trembles
> in the autumn breeze.

October poured through the aspens and over the rocks. I stared into the far distance, then looked down at the page. The haiku was written by Buson.

I vowed then and there, in that northern New Mexico

hot springs, that if I ever went to Japan again I'd find Buson's grave and pay homage.

It took nineteen years before I had the opportunity to fulfill my vow.

Sawdust, Gruel, and Mochi

I plan to leave for Japan on October 29. But when the time comes, I don't want to leave home. In all my decades in New Mexico, I've never seen a more gorgeous fall. The aspens and cottonwoods along Alameda, following the thin Santa Fe River and down Acequia Madre, are pure gold. New Mexico does not get the red and orange of eastern autumns, only a rich dash of crimson from the ivy crawling up and entwining tree limbs and trunks. But this yellow is enough. We even have some hard rains in this dry country, the air sweet. The leaves do not fall but continue to glimmer week after week, stretching out every inch of this season.

I hadn't had a regular old café for doing writing practice in for a long time. Mostly I write in the small studio attached to my house and surrender to solitude. But I recently discovered Capitol Coffee, on the corner of Old Santa Fe Trail and Paseo de Peralta, next to Kaune's, the local grocer, and I am in heaven, with the comfortable wooden chairs like they had in public schools long ago, square tables, big windows, across from the state capitol. A blue US mailbox on the corner, where mail is picked up once a day at 1:10 (I have a habit of sending postcards to friends). Even the stretch of parking lot outside seems beautiful. God's country. I am writing in my glory. Here I am again, with people chatting around me and Dylan blasting over the loudspeakers.

I don't want to leave the café and that towering cotton-wood at the top curve of the hill, each leaf a glittering gilt heart. Right before I leave for the airport, I run out of my house a last time to look.

I fly to Osaka the next day and arrive the day after that. Eleven hours over the ocean once I make it to San Francisco.

Mitsue, a Japanese student from Upaya who I'd become friends with, and who has been in the West for twelve years, meets me at the airport. She is also to be the guide on the part of my trip that is with Upaya Zen Center and led by my friends Joan Halifax and Kaz Tanahashi. Joan is a Zen teacher whose zendo was just up the road from me in Santa Fe; Kaz is a writer, translator, calligraphy master, and nearly lifelong Zen practitioner.

I've come several days earlier than the formal two-week tour, because I want to spend time in Osaka. *Why Osaka?* people asked. The second-largest city in Japan, a business center, the economic drive of the country, shooting up tall buildings, considered a place of little charm.

My Zen teacher, Katagiri Roshi, was born in Osaka in 1928, the youngest of seven children, and lived there till he was five. His family thought he would become a priest, because as a young boy he loved to chew incense. I know the city has changed and would be unrecognizable today to those who lived in old Osaka, but I am sure that somehow I will be able to feel its original flavor. I want to taste where he was born.

I've changed a lot since studying with Katagiri almost thirty years ago, but I still want to understand the man who was my great teacher. I've also noticed that many Japanese writers I admired were born in or connected to Osaka. Buson was born here, and Basho died here. Also *The Makioka Sisters*, a novel I love, written in the 1940s by Tanizaki, takes place mostly in Osaka.

On the bus from the airport to the hotel, Mitsue tells me, "Three weeks ago, I was in a small town up north — Takayama — and met someone who read your book." *Writing Down the Bones* is the only one of my books that has been translated into Japanese. "He'd like to meet you."

In a jet-lag blur, I watch signs in kanji snap past the window as the bus moves through the industrial outskirts of the city. I am not terribly interested in meeting a writing student. I say, "Okay. Tell him we can connect for an hour at the end of our trip in three and a half weeks, when we return to Kyoto, maybe that evening. Can he meet us there?"

It is an outlandish plan — too long a time away and too far from Takayama. *He'll never come*, I think.

"Okay. I'll email him." Mitsue pulls out her tablet computer.

I've forgotten the whole thing by the time we arrive at my hotel.

The mattress is firm. The bathroom is equipped with all kinds of controls for lighting up the mirror, the bath, the sink. The toilet seat is heated: press one button and your bottom is cleaned, press another and your front is sprayed. Near the door is a switch: *Want maid service? Don't want it?* A button by my bed closes the curtains. Ahh, the Japanese. I fall into a deep sleep below any time zone.

Early the next morning I call down to the front desk.

"Do you speak English?" I ask.

"Yes."

"What is the weather, the temperature?"

A long pause. The receptionist doesn't understand my question.

I am passed to two other people.

"Call back," the third one says.

Ten minutes later the phone rings. "I don't know," the man at the other end recites. Don't know English or the weather? I give up and look out from the twenty-sixth floor, trying to discern what people below are wearing. All I can tell is that they are wearing long sleeves.

At an outdoor café, I sit at a small round table with hard silver chairs, a row of just-planted ginkgoes nearby, and watch passersby on the street. Some wear white masks — in Japan if you are sick, you wear a mask. How civilized. No one seems in a rush, and a sparkling happiness pervades this thriving city. So many young, stylish people in groups of ones, twos, and threes. I am not a shoe person but cannot help but notice the shoes on their feet. Boots, buckles, straps, purple, red, turquoise, and all moving at a comfortable gait. One girl has a cloth bag with *Miel* written on it. Kitty-corner to this café is a McDonald's: two stories, demure, with the logo placed on the curved corner of the building to fit in with the ambience here. McDonald's adapts — in New Mexico they serve their hamburgers in adobe-like constructions. Across the street is Maruzen & Junkudo, a seven-story independent bookstore. The sixth floor houses English books and puts any American bookstore to shame. It has the full collection of the Modern Library and a row of English literature in Korean, French, Russian, and Japanese.

Nearby is the Yodo River, wide as the Mississippi. I plan to meet up with everyone else for the group trip on Monday. Today is Friday. I treasure the private pleasure of these days.

Last night I had a vague dream about my father, who fought the Japanese in World War II. I felt him hovering over me, dead fourteen years, trying to tell me something, how it is simply to be alive and then to die. The Japanese were under a death oath the entire time they were in the war. *A sociology of death.* "The Japanese were great soldiers," my father contended.

I suspected that in some inverse way I came to Japan to be closer to my father, to his generation, but I couldn't look straight at World War II's European devastation, with its concentration camps. Instead I traveled to view the old enemy, seeing our reflection from another angle, to stand on Japanese shores and look back over my shoulder, from the country that joined with Germany to dominate the world. I'd been to Japan fourteen years earlier, in 1998, but back then I was still idealistic, searching out Zen practice in remote temples.

The Japanese held the same dream for Asia that the Germans had for the West, believing they were the superior race. The Chinese and Koreans would be their slaves. The Japanese fought on the side of the people who created the ovens and gassed Jews. But one of their people, Dainin Katagiri, had given me the deepest practice into my essential nature, the way to peace, in a zendo in the Midwest.

Katagiri was born two years before his imperialist country began its long war in 1931 with what they called the Manchurian Incident — the invasion of China, resulting in mass murder. The Japanese military thought the Chinese didn't count as people. Then in 1932 the Japanese began conflicts with Russia. By the time of its surrender in 1945, Japan was starving. The imperial ruler sent out notices on how to eat sawdust. This was a bit of the atmosphere in which Katagiri grew up.

After the war, as a young man, Katagiri practiced deep in the forested mountains at Eihe-ji Monastery, the practice center for Soto Zen. During that time he must have heard much talk of America. Who were the Americans? Were they really monsters, as the Japanese were told during the war? He was an earnest, serious student. Could he plant what he was learning, a seed of peace and truth, in this new country that seemed optimistic and full of hope? Zen in Japan at that time was mostly used for funeral ceremonies. Few people practiced the Way or had interest in it. They had already suffered enough. Zen was too hard. The Japanese were interested in restoring their country. During the war, many Zen teachers had aligned with the emperor, using Zen principles as a justification for war. Katagiri told stories about being in the monastery and having only hot water with a few grains of rice floating in it, calling it a thin gruel.

After the war, the United States, under MacArthur, demanded that Japan become democratic. For centuries the people had been ruled by the landowners, the emperor, and the powerful, pugnacious military. Now each person should vote. They turned their surprising energy, even after being broken from years of war, to the task of pleasing MacArthur, the US commander in charge of the defeated country.

Mitsue rides the train in from her parents' place in the suburbs and meets me at noon in the hotel lobby. Typical of the hospitable Japanese, she is concerned about meeting my need to get a sense of old Osaka. She conferred with her parents, who were impressed that I was interested in Buson, an honored traditional Japanese writer.

"How about the zoo? They must have one here," I say as soon as I see Mitsue. I am trusting an odd hunch. Yes, I have the prejudice that all animal lovers have — that we should quit catching and caging them. I hadn't been to a zoo in at least forty years, yet one of my fondest memories is spending a full day with my father at the Bronx Zoo when I was ten.

Mitsue's head jerks back in surprise — she has a full itinerary planned for us. Then a broad smile spreads across her face. "Let me look up where it could be." She too is discovering Japan after living abroad for so long.

As soon as we step into the old zoo on the outskirts of

Osaka, we know we are in the right place. In a tank before us is not a whale or a shark but a pink hippo, huge as an American trailer, swimming under water. Mitsue and I look at each other with our mouths hanging open and then turn back to gaze at this strange animal, clearly buoyant and in his own elemental dream. Who cares about a search for meaning or a haiku poet's grave? We are right in the amazing, fat moment before us.

We move on to the next exhibit, a large, open plain with a tall standing tree in the distance. We lower our sight: under the tree is a black rhino, standing still, prehistoric, dusty as though in driest Africa. We drift over to the plaque explaining this animal's habits. A bit of it is in English, about how the rhino steps in his own feces and with it marks his territory.

We gaze at the black rhino for a long time, that steady stance on four substantial legs, his tough-leather gray hide, the unblinking eyes and curved horn above his nose. He is in the wrong place and wrong time but still surviving.

I excuse myself to use the public bathroom. Like my hotel bathroom, here is a heated seat and a side panel with buttons for spraying yourself. Mitsue told me this toilet refinement is new since she left the country. Before, in winter they didn't have central heating, and homes were quite frigid. I remembered Roshi talking of the coal burner in the monastery under the low table when they had tea; otherwise, there was no heat, and the wet cold was penetrating. At the time I thought this was exclusive to monks' lives. I am beginning to understand that Zen life and Japanese life are closely entwined.

"At first in the West, I couldn't get used to heat all the time, all over the room," Mitsue explains. "But then I loved it."

I find Mitsue and we move on to the lions' den. Two females are splayed out on rocks in the pale sun, and a male with a ragged mane restlessly struts through long reeds.

Mitsue points something out to me — and it seems important to her. The male, when he walks below a hanging branch of a small tree, takes evident pleasure in the top of a leaf running across his face. She repeats the sight of it twice.

A cougar beside a jaguar — we can barely tell the difference between them since they're both spotted, small-faced, lean, muscled, and active, jumping from mound to mound. Then a squirrel in a small cage. At first I figure he crawled out of a tree to get some nuts, but no. Japan does not have squirrels like this. This animal is an oddity to be peered at, like a koala from Australia.

We pass through a section of concession stands on bumpy, cracked sidewalks — pretzels, green candy cotton, cans of green tea, all signs in kanji. This zoo is an old place with a casual, relaxed feeling.

A two-humped camel, and then two kangaroos.

"I've never seen one hop," Mitsue says, leaning over the rail.

"Let's wait until they do," but we only see them use their short front legs to bend and move forward.

As we are about to give up, one hops quickly out of sight — and then the other. Holding the rail, Mitsue leans back with her face in the weak sun. "We finally saw it."

"Let's sit zazen." I motion to an old bench.

Mitsue's eyes open wide. "Right here?"

"Sure." I shove my purse to my back for support and get comfortable. Mitsue straightens her back and exhales slowly. Not having a bell, I call out, "Ding, ding, ding." We settle in for half an hour among the animals.

We breathe and listen to their thin cries and yelps, then a tinny tune repeated over the sound system. Couples stroll by, holding hands. Mothers push carriages. Older children skip ahead. All under the old twisted cherry trees lining the path, not blooming on this first day of November.

I imagine a young Katagiri walking these streets and feel close to the man who eventually gave me this practice of following my breath, all the way out, then the instant of no longer exhaling, out there in the emptiness, just before turning around, bringing the breath back into me.

An attendant on a white bike rides by and announces, "Closing in a half hour."

"Ding," my voice rings out, at five to five.

The zoo is already empty, but no way can we rush to the exit. We are outside of time. We pass the white monkey house and Mitsue tries the door. No entry.

The attendant locks the gate to the zoo the moment we step outside.

Across the street, we stride down narrow alleys lined with stalls, open-air shops, lightbulbs dangling high up across walkways on wires. The Japanese love electricity.

Basically, I like to eat what my grandmother served: lots of chicken, mashed potatoes put back in the skin, lamb chops, strudel, an occasional serving of peas or green beans, apple-sauce and coleslaw made from scratch. I have graduated to kale, avocados, butter lettuce, even sushi on occasion, but take me to a Chinese restaurant, and I humbly look down the menu for shrimp fried rice.

Also, I don't drink alcohol. That means no sake. I took vows with Thich Nhat Hanh, the Vietnamese Buddhist monk, in 1990 not to drink. In 1967 he came to the States to beg us to stop bombing his country. He thought the fact that no bombs were being dropped in America would render it a peaceful place, so he was surprised to feel such suffering here. He looked deeply and saw that one core problem was alcoholism. It was tearing families apart. He asked people who studied with him not to support alcohol either by buying or drinking it.

For thirty years my father owned a tavern. He'd let old drunks in the back door at 7:30 AM for their first drink. He paid for many of his customers' burials. My family's liveli-hood was dependent on others' suffering. I hadn't drunk al-cohol since I was in my forties.

I point to a pancake place that looks safe, and Mitsue pronounces the name of the restaurant: Doyasa. We enter the dark, narrow space. A long counter, empty at this early eve-ning hour.

We sit down on stools at the bar. Mitsue speaks brisk Jap-anese to the two men, black bandannas with knots in the back tied around their heads.

I nudge her. "Ask them if there's wheat in the pancakes." I started having problems digesting gluten a decade earlier.

Much talk back and forth. "He'll make it mostly with vegetables and fish. Doesn't know what's in the batter."

"Okay." Then I have another question: "Ask him where the fish comes from." The night before I left, my dear friend Wendy had called. "Natalie, swear to me you won't eat fish. They're all contaminated from the Fukushima reactor leak. Mayumi was just in from Japan. She's trying to shut down the plant." She wouldn't let me off the phone until I promised. "Also, stay away from chicken. Eat only vegetables."

I hear an imperceptible sigh issue from Mitsue's lips and her chest sinks slightly. She would never say *no* or *Natalie, enough. This is embarrassing.*

Instead, another spry interaction ensues, plus some chuckling. I blush, the quintessential American tourist. "He says no worry. Fish comes from far away." I think *probably frozen* but shut up.

The pancake is delicious.

We leave the restaurant in the dark, and the narrow passages are livelier. People have gotten out of work. We turn a corner, where a father and son are about to close their very old mochi shop, but they let us in to taste this fresh rare, soft, special sweet made with rice flour and bean paste and kneaded repeatedly. I take a bite and my tongue experiences something almost incandescent, lit from within. I close my eyes. Give me the right thing, and who says I can't cross borders?

I feel lively and free in this city that has an inferiority complex: Tokyo is bigger and Kyoto is the old capital. Here they knock down old buildings to build tall skyscrapers, but the streets are filled with a lively, hip energy, and you feel anything new can happen alongside good haircuts and stylish, colorful clothes.

You can feel the optimism, the belief in economy and effort. The people in Osaka do not leave Osaka. They say, *We are better here. Steady, stable, open, friendly, secure.*

The next day we take the train to Kyoto. We still have a day before the rest of the traveling group joins us. We plan to visit the place where Buson's house stood. Later, at the end of the trip, I intend to find and visit his grave.

Mitsue takes me to the spot marked by a wooden plaque on a busy street in the center of Kyoto where Buson lived. I cannot read the kanji, but Mitsue translates the formal history and dates. Next to the wooden plaque stands a cement marker, encasing the spot in a more durable form.

At our backs on the narrow street, a boy bicycles by; two young girls giggle. An old woman carries a bag of groceries with green onion tops hanging out the top. I put my cheek next to the transient wood of the marker, happy that Buson was honored in the middle of this human world of getting and spending.

Full and Shattered Bowls

In Santa Fe I recited Buson's haiku to a friend:

> Ah, grief and sadness!
> The fishing line trembles
> in the autumn breeze

She acknowledged how beautiful it was. Then she said, "I don't believe it's Buson's. You wrote it."

I laughed. Of course I hadn't, but I understood. When someone carries something for so long it becomes theirs. There is no Buson anymore. Or you are Buson. You carry him and the lineage forward.

Really, this is how we learn to write. We fall in love with an author and realize we are what we love. No separation.

The next morning at our Kyoto hotel, Mitsue and I eat our breakfast with a woman who will be on the group trip, which is starting the next evening. Ulrike reminds me that we practiced together with Richard Baker, in the mid-1980s in Santa Fe, when I returned from my years in Minnesota studying with Katagiri Roshi. I've already gobbled down my meal, so I watch her eat the small dish of scrambled eggs and white yogurt, spread the apple jelly on her toast, and then sip a yellow soup with a green leaf of some sort floating in it.

The bare years flicker back, and the smoke of recognition drifts across my mind. Her blonde hair, straight nose, her attention marked with the slight cock of her head. We did not converse much back then, but she knew people I knew: Robert Winson, who died too young; Philip Whalen, the poet; Miriam Bobkoff, the priest who worked in the library. Across the small table, Ulrike and I eye each other with a deep recognition.

Ulrike tells me about Yasunari Kawabata and his last novel, *Beauty and Sadness*, about a middle-aged writer who returns to Kyoto to seek an old lover who is now a famous painter and living with a woman. "It has everything in it," she says.

Then we talk of *The Book of Tea* by Okakura Kakuzo, written in 1906. Of how tea was developed among nobles and peasants, how it was first boiled, later whipped, and still later steeped. Then how tea developed over time into an art form, almost a Zen practice of aestheticism. "The book makes me enjoy the tea even more," Ulrike says.

In the late morning we go on a short walk away from our cozy, relaxed, half-hippie ryokan to a temple established in 1605 by a noblewoman, in memory of her late husband, Toyotomi Hideyoshi, the last daimyo, before the dynasty shoguns took over.

It's raining. We huddle under our black umbrellas as we climb the long stairs to the Kodai-ji Temple complex. We wander over wooden bridges and narrow paths through Japanese maples, past green moss growing on rocks. Beside us are bamboo groves and camellias shyly opening pink buds.

Ulrike wants to see the teahouse here, designed by Sen no Rikyu, the ultimate tea master, the man who simplified the tea ceremony by using rustic items made in Japan rather than fancy, expensive tools from China. At the age of sixty-one he became Hideyoshi's tea master, and their relationship quickly deepened. Here Rikyu's influence flowered, popularizing the philosophy of *wabi-sabi*, finding beauty in the simple and elemental, in things imperfect, incomplete — a cracked cup, or caring for the flower container, tea scoop, lid rest — and in one's surroundings, an awareness of the incense wafting through the room, the shudder of leaves outside, the singing kettle, the gray stone lanterns along the path.

Halfway through our walk we come upon the teahouse, a small square building with exposed wooden structural elements and a second floor. I feel as though we've entered inner Japan — the Japan of carefully placed stones and small trimmed shrubs that look like clouds. The perfect sense of *sabi*, subtle, always-present impermanence, the passing of seasons, and its exquisite perception of longing, loneliness, and surrender.

Although Rikyu was one of his closest confidants, Hideyoshi grew jealous of his popularity and influence. When Rikyu disagreed with his lord's idea of invading Korea, Hideyoshi, an arrogant despot, distrustful even of his closest comrade, ordered him to commit ritual suicide. His friends begged Rikyu to wait a little bit — maybe Hideyoshi would reconsider? But Rikyu was austerely loyal and said that his death might do some good by encouraging Hideyoshi to reconsider the invasion.

Rikyu's last act was to hold an exquisite, severe tea ceremony. And after each guest downed their bowl of tea, he presented in ritual etiquette each tea instrument for examination. Then he offered each of his guests a piece of the ceremonial instruments as a remembrance — except the bowl. This he shattered, uttering, "Never again shall this bowl, polluted by the lips of misfortune, be used by man." The guests departed with difficulty, saying their last farewells. But one, Rikyu's nearest and dearest, was asked to remain and witness his end.

Rikyu then removed his tea gown and folded it. Underneath he was wearing an immaculate white death robe. Seeking to be in harmony with the great rhythm of the universe, Rikyu prepared to enter the unknown. He uttered his last words, a death poem addressed to the dagger, "sword of eternity...thy has cleft thy way." Then, with a smile on his face, he plunged the dagger into his belly.

Within a year, Hideyoshi expressed his remorse.

The rain starts to pound and bounce off surfaces. Visitors run for cover from the driving storm. Ulrike and I find a small teahouse on the grounds with a roof and two walls. Looking out at the gardens through the veil of the downpour, we sit low on a tatami at a narrow table. We are the only ones here. We are served big black bowls of whipped green tea, very hot, with a single almond cookie the size of a fifty-cent piece. We drink the tea quickly. I want more tea, more cookies, but at the same time appreciate the beauty of *just enough, just this,* complete sufficiency.

As I sit gazing at the garden, I contemplate the great coincidence of crossing paths with a person I sat with in the silent zendo so many years earlier. How the movement of planets and stars, the revolving of the Earth, have brought us face-to-face. The two of us in Japan, unplanned, together.

Ulrike was the youngest woman in Germany to receive her PhD in molecular biology from the Max Planck Institute. As we talk we discover we both had demanding mothers who gave little but wanted lots of devotion. Mine has been dead five years. Hers has been on the brink of death for a long time. She has a brother, who is a medical doctor, dedicated to keeping her mother alive.

The rain stops. Ulrike goes outside to photograph the teahouse and to use the bathroom. I wait under the shelter and look out at rain-soaked clipped hedges, low, slow gray clouds, a walking bridge over a pond near a bamboo grove. My damp fingers are wrapped around the empty tea bowl. I'm hearing the drip drip drip of rain off the eaves hitting the close-shaved grass, and looking out at the wet, shining pebble path. Time becomes thick, steamy, and luxurious.

An old, brief love affair of many years ago comes to mind. I wonder where she is now?

I think: *Who knows what my last thoughts will be right before I die? Maybe something inconsequential like how my uncle Sam taught me to tie a bow one summer evening on our back patio, bent over my shoe, when I was eight.*

Ulrike returns. "Rikyu has meant so much to me. I had not looked for him. It was like I was found by him."

It begins to drizzle again.

A cold rain starting
and no hat —
so?

BASHO

The next day I search for a bookstore in Kyoto to find Kawabata, the novelist Ulrike told me about. They have only one book by this Japanese Nobel Prize winner: an English version of *The Old Capital*. I purchase it.

Snow Falls

Issa is another of Allen Ginsberg's declared greats. Basho is revered, but Issa is loved for his humor, his humanity, his compassion.

I have learned to distinguish one haiku writer from another. Even in three short lines, each has their unique awareness, and pain, and personal history.

Issa lived from 1762 to 1826 and came of age after Buson died. He earned his place in haiku through a life of suffering. In comparison, Basho's and Buson's haiku lives seem to have developed in relative comfort.

Issa's mother died when he was three years old. He wrote his first haiku when he was six:

> Come play with me!
> You, little sparrow
> Motherless sparrow!

His stepmother was cruel to him, so he left home at fourteen, only returning, two decades later, for his father's funeral. Although he was the main heir of the family house and land, his stepmother and half brother kept him from the property for thirteen more years. When he finally returned again to his village and was able to claim his inheritance, he met and married a local woman. They had four children, but none of them survived for long, dying one by one from diseases such as smallpox, and, in one case, accidental suffocation. Especially devastating to Issa was the death of his daughter Sato, in 1819, inspiring one of his most poignant verses:

> The world of dew
> is only a world of dew —
> and yet

Here's another:

> In a dream
> my daughter lifts a melon
> to her soft cheek

A few years later his wife died. The following year he married again but divorced within three months. Two years later he married his third wife.

Three years later, his familial house burned down in a fire that swept through his village. This was the final blow for Issa. He and his wife moved into a small, musty grain barn for the remaining months of his life. He died shortly before his third wife gave birth to another longed-for daughter.

This single haiku expresses his life's trajectory:

Oh, autumn winds
tell me where I'm bound,
which particular hell

Yet his familial tragedies were not the whole story of his life. After leaving home early, he resurfaced as a member of a haiku school in his twenties, adopting the pen name Issa, meaning "cup of tea." The wounded, unwanted stepson had found poetry and dedicated his life to the Way of haiku.

go ahead, make love!
make love!
summer cicadas

Thus spring begins: old
stupidities repeated,
new errors invented

Inspired by Basho, Issa took to the road on writing journeys and committed himself to exploring all his moods in haiku. During this time he also found Buddhism, and as an artist full of compassion and respect for all beings, large and small, he honored their integrity in his work:

sitting on her eggs
the chicken admires
the peony

if someone comes
change into frogs!
cooling melons

Get out, little sparrow!
Get out of the way!
Mr. Horse is coming

People recognized Issa as a democratic person, defend-
ing the underdog, transforming suffering into acceptance and
humor.

Fleas in my hut
it's my fault
you look so skinny

His reputation spread, and he enjoyed celebrity even
during his hard years.

The pampas grass
waves good-by, good-by
to departing autumn

Yet, whatever the emotion, Issa fully faced what was in
front of him.

My dear old village,
every memory of home
pierces like a thorn

Mother, I weep
for you as I watch the sea
each time I watch the sea

Mountain persimmons;
the mother is eating
the astringent parts

I wish she were here
to listen to my bitching
and enjoy this moon

For thirty-five years I have carried around a small red booklet, *Inch by Inch: 45 Haiku* by Issa, translated by Nanao Sakaki, a wandering Japanese poet. Here's a paragraph from the short introduction: "Not gifted with genius, but honestly holding his experience deep in his heart, he kept his simplicity and humanity."

Who can be
a stranger
under the cherry blossoms?

These few lines Nanao wrote nail Issa. I have read them over and over as inspiration.

First lightning bug this year
why do you turn away?
It's me, Issa!

Pissing, pissing
down there
an iris blooming

Just as he is
he goes to bed and gets up
the snail —

Flies, fleas, mosquitos
and people — all long lived
in my poor village

And the last one in this old collection, the back cover torn
off long ago:

Simply, I'm here
simply, snow falls

Water, Earth, Light

Mitsue wakes me with a phone call just before dinner. I napped too long in late afternoon and missed the formal introduction to the group traveling together.

I dash to the lobby and quickly meet twenty-six fellow travelers. One has a big cast on her leg. At age fifty-five, she is taking her first trip out of the US — and she broke her ankle a week earlier. She isn't going to let anything stop her. I meet several couples and a good smattering of individuals who are sharing rooms with fellow travelers they've never met before. (I have opted for my own room.) Our group includes doctors and nurses who work in hospice; a retired engineer; an Australian man without his wife; a redheaded young Southerner with her husband, who survived tongue cancer; another Southerner married to a Frenchman, who declares on the first night that he hates tofu; yet another Southerner who has been to Japan many times already; and a tough retired state district attorney.

For more than thirty years Kaz and Joan have taken a group to Japan; each year the trip has a different Buddhist orientation. This year the trip focuses on visiting Buddhist sites but will also include the island of Naoshima, known in Japan as "the art island." Naoshima isn't particularly connected to Buddhism or Zen, but Joan and Kaz decided to throw in something wonderful.

I sense that none of us, not even Joan or Kaz, has broken the code of Japan and that we are all beginners, even Kaz, who is Japanese but has lived in the West for more than forty years.

Joan's returning year after year to Japan has led to her work in compassion and end-of-life care, first established in the United States and Europe, with a national organization studied all over Japan, creating a revolution in Japanese health care. I vaguely know about this work of hers — at home we hike together in the surrounding mountains and hills — yet I intuit the importance of what she is doing and feel proud of her.

As we ride the bus to our first destination, I read Kawabata's bio at the back of his novel. He was born in Osaka, another writer connected to the place. I also read that he committed suicide in 1972. It's as if we writers can write the truth but not bear to live with it.

We file out at the entrance to Ryoan-ji Temple, a UNESCO world heritage site. Kaz smiles at us and says, "There are fifteen stones, but wherever you stand you can only see fourteen of them. It's a mystery." Then he adds, "Like life. Always present is an unknown element."

A long path takes us to an inner courtyard, where people are crowded around a large rectangular plot of white pebbles surrounding an arrangement of large stones. The stones stand erect, in small groups.

I count fourteen. I change positions. Still only fourteen. I shift and try again — and again. Same result. I stop trying and plop down on the edge of the platform, among many school-children. At our backs are a bamboo grove and running water, but before us is this cold void of a garden, with not one green plant, flower, pond, or walkway.

Soon I grow restless and jump up, go to a side alcove. There I page through books about this garden in German, French, Chinese, Korean, thinking I'll find some clue in a language I don't understand. *Perfect*, I think. *I'm totally annoyed.*

On this trip I am mostly being taken to places I am not familiar with. I was sent an itinerary when I registered, but I didn't research any of the destinations. I prefer to meet something straight on, in ignorance. I like a backward journey, not looking too much ahead. So I deserve the annoyance I feel at Ryoan-ji. But I know from past experience that this is how I absorb encounters — through feeling the texture of my own resistance.

In that first week, we visit a long list of Zen temples I cannot name. One marks the transmission of Zen from China to Japan; one is where a great monk brought the Heart Sutra to the homeland. One night we eat a nine-course meal dedicated to autumn. Red maple leaves are placed subtly, coquettishly, on plates and bowls. We lift chopsticks, then place them aside and bring the soup bowls to our mouths. Over and over, we sip sour tea and sweet tea. We bow and awkwardly repeat, "*Arigatou gozaimasu.*" Later, we learn to add *domo* and to smile.

I often feel like a klutz in my hiking boots, sitting or

standing next to the Japanese women in their delicate foot-wear, watching them giggle behind their hands.

Kaz stands in the aisle at the front of the chartered bus, ex-plaining Japanese Buddhist history. We strain to hear his soft voice through the loud hum of the engine as we barrel through the unknown landscape. "Edwin Reischauer saved Kyoto. He was an American born in Tokyo to missionaries and lived in Japan as a young man. Later, back in the US, during World War II, Reischauer was on the committee to decide which cities to drop the new bomb on. When Kyoto was named as a possibility, Reischauer burst out sobbing. The serious, stern committee men took note and crossed the old capital off the list."

After four trains, two buses, and one ferry ride, we arrive in the town of Miyajima, where we must double up in tradi-tional ryokan rooms, sleeping on futons on the floor. I share a room with Ulrike, and we talk late into the night, lights out, windows open to the sea below. We talk seriously, earnestly, about who we are, how we became who we are, and our ded-ication to Zen practice though living in the world. The words pour out of us into the sticky room and cool night.

The next morning, we wake early. Ulrike puts on her kimono and announces, "I'm going down to the women's baths."

Why do that? I think. The tub in our room looks deep and luxurious. But I trail after her, towel over my shoulder, clomping behind in wooden sandals.

The elevator drops through the floors till we are below the building. The pool outside is beside a fast, cold stream sided by smooth rocks. The two of us fall into an immediate silence and step into unspeakably hot water. We are the only ones there.

Here again is the Japan we are looking for. As I slip into the water, I fall below the line of thought.

There I suddenly feel my old friend Katherine Thanas, who died less than two years earlier. There's no interchange; I just feel her presence. Katherine was eighty-five, the retired abbot of Santa Cruz Zen Center, when she fell in her modest apartment, hit her head, and died a week later. No thought of how strange for her to show up here. Why not? It's a lovely place, especially now that Katherine has passed beyond boundaries.

I look up. Ulrike is across the pool in her own dream. Her long back goes in and out of the water. We stay submerged and silent for an unbroken, everlasting amount of time.

Two hours later, wandering the winding streets of town, I run into the young redheaded woman from our tour. Instantly, I flash back to the last time I saw her, early yesterday morning. As our group waited for a train, her husband kissed her long and hungrily on the lips. I couldn't help watching. Just the lips lingering, nothing else touching. His head bent toward hers.

I find a coffee shop and go inside. Beans in bags, a chocolate cake on display. Here I spend most of the afternoon, writing in my notebook. I order cake and coffee, then a second piece of cake. I'd go back to Japan just to write there again.

A couple from our group wanders in. "Order the cake," I whisper to them.

Later, as the rain pours down, I pass a small, empty restaurant with plastic models of food choices for louts like me who can't read kanji. Shrimp fried rice is displayed. It's what I want for lunch. I go in and order. Dare I say it? It is my most enjoyable meal of the whole trip. I can still see the yellow walls of the room, the lace curtains, the rain dripping down the big windows, the faux Chinese food. Forgive me, my gourmet friends. I am happy unto myself.

The next day we ferry back, then take two trains and two more ferries. A train station melds into a bus station. Our group is in a good-natured trance. Then, in one bright moment, the young couple has another long public kiss that stops time.

We arrive at the Benesse House on Naoshima, the art island. We are herded into a conference room and seated at long tables. The director starts to give us all a lecture. I think, *If I don't get out of here, I'm going to scream. Don't give me information ahead of experience.*

I jump up and say I need to lie down. I hold the back of my hand to my forehead for effect, as though fainting is imminent.

Somebody rushes me out of the room and down a long hall, past many numbered doors, to my room, a long, narrow space with a wide balcony.

I take a long, hot bath in a deep tub. Wrapped in a white terry bathrobe the hotel provides, I look around the room. I think, *This is probably the most intelligent hotel room I've ever been in.* Minimal but conscious; a good bed; good lighting; beautiful wood; a small refrigerator; a large amber bar of soap with a plastic bag beside it, to take home the diminished soap bar as a memento; wood slats that open and close in front of the windows.

A knock at my door. It's Roshi Joan. She sits at the small table, and we both go on about our rooms and how lovely it is to be here together. "Look at this." I hold up a comb, a pad, a bottle of water, a corner of my bathrobe. I point to the sink, the desk. I swirl around the room.

Roshi laughs, leaning her head back, relaxed and happy, enjoying my joy, this woman who also has opened the door wider for Japanese Buddhists in their own country, teaching them the importance of social engagement, to reach where suffering is prevalent and not noticed.

> Snowstorm at the Refuge
> strange joy to see
> the world disappear
> JOAN HALIFAX

Before the introduction of the internet, Soichiro Fukutake made his fortune in publishing and in correspondence education, especially the teaching of language through the mail.

His company sold old-style, personal booklets and lessons for kids in schools and nurseries, and also for the aged. Fukutake's company served people of every age.

But Fukutake's son had his own vision. He hired Tadao Ando, the innovative, number one architect in Japan, to create a "living museum" — actually, a group of norm-shattering museums — on the island of Naoshima, where few people lived. He named his living museums Benesse, from the Latin word that means "to be good, well blessed." We are here to see these museums: art in fresh dimensions.

Our first stop the next day is the Chichu Art Museum. The word *museum* conjures up walls of paintings or open spaces with sculptures. Chichu blows the top off any preconception we have about what a museum is. Inside the building, we snake and wander. Constructed in 2004, most of the space is underground. Yet it receives an abundance of natural light. Three artists dedicated to working with light have their work on permanent display.

One of the artists, James Turrell, has large simultaneous exhibits in New York, Houston, and Los Angeles while we are here. I sit in a round room underground, gazing up through a big opening at the sky. No explanation. Just look. I remember a while back reading that the shifting light effects of his "skyspaces" reveal his philosophy: "We are dwellers at the bottom of an ocean of air. We create the color and shape of the sky. It does not exist outside the self."

Since 1975 Turrell has worked on a land art project in Arizona, outside Flagstaff, taking a four-hundred-thousand-year-old volcanic crater and making it into an integrated naked-eye observatory and visual art display. The installation consists of twenty underground rooms, each designed to alter our perception of light from the sun, moon, and stars. Turrell plays with the way the light enters our eyeballs. Each way you turn provides another utterly new impression.

We move in groups of five from one Turrell experience to another. Shoes off; shoes on. Attendants in white gloves in the background ask us to be quiet, to wait, to go.

On another level the size of a gymnasium, Walter De Maria has created twenty-seven golden geometric forms. Depending on the time of day, the space dramatically changes under the natural light coming in from the ceiling. The title of the work is *Seen/Unseen Known/Unknown*. The title fits the experience perfectly.

Walter De Maria also created the long-term installation *The Earth Room* on Wooster Street in New York City, which happened to be in the same building as my poetry publisher, the Overlook Press. The room is filled with about two feet of dirt. You don't enter the room; you stand at the entrance and stare. There is no entry fee. And it's so out of place, on the second floor of a city office building. De Maria actually gets the viewer to consider *dirt*.

Eventually we are guided down to the lowest level, where I stand in speechless, open-mouthed awe — the third artist is Monet. Hanging in an intimate gallery are five large paintings of water lilies that Monet painted at the gardens he created in Giverny, an hour outside Paris. Monet painted these later in his life, after his second wife died and his oldest son, Jean, also died, in 1914. World War I was raging in Europe. He felt alone, shattered, and defeated. He would go to the pond and sit before the water lilies in despair. How to capture what was before him? Under his deft hand, the lilies broke open, filled with more light, became more abstract, the world no longer a solid place.

In the early twentieth century, on flat canvases, Monet did just what the other two artists are doing — captured light.

———

The Chichu Museum is just the beginning. There are installations throughout the island.

Next I enter an astounding museum, also designed by Tadao Ando, dedicated to the work of Lee Ufan, a Korean artist who lives in Japan and Paris. I take pleasure in the austerity of his paintings — one brush mark along a white canvas, one stroke in the center of another.

I feel an extraordinary presence in that one stroke, and daring. No need to entertain, to fill the canvas with conversation.

I can hear my father: *Oh, I could do that.*

No, you couldn't, I mentally tell him, reaching back through the years beyond his death.

At the small museum gift shop, I purchase two postcards of Ufan's austere works. They are a gift for one of my students, who has a PhD in art history. I'll hand them to her and simply say, "Naoshima." I won't try to describe anything.

This Is Impossible

We take a boat to Inujima, an island where an old copper refinery ran from 1909 to 1919. In 2008 it became the center of a large-scale art project dedicated to the writer Yukio Mishima.

Before coming to Japan, I read John Nathan's biography of Mishima, who wrote thirty-four novels, fifty plays, and short stories and essays. He was nominated for a Nobel Prize in Literature three times, but in 1968, when it was given to Kawabata — the first Japanese writer ever to receive it — he realized that his chances of ever getting it were slim.

After World War II Mishima was concerned that in Japan's rush to modernize and catch up with the West, the true spirit and culture of the country were being lost. He became more and more a right-wing radical. He was incensed that Emperor Hirohito, who represented the essence and divinity of Japan, had surrendered. Millions of Japanese had died for him as their living god — all in vain.

Mishima formed the Shield Society, a private militia of students in the martial arts. The Shield Society's sworn ideal was to bring Japan back to its prewar ways and to reinstitute the emperor as a symbol of its greatness. In 1970, at the age of forty-five, Mishima attempted a coup with four other Shield Society members. They took over the Tokyo headquarters of the Japan Self-Defense Forces, barricaded the office, and tied the commander to his chair. Holding a prepared manifesto, Mishima stepped out onto the balcony and addressed the soldiers, who jeered and laughed at him.

After his speech — this part had been planned for at least a year — he committed traditional samurai seppuku, disemboweling himself.

As part of the ceremony, his second in command stepped forward to sever Mishima's head but failed several times. Another member of the four completed it. Then the first officer who failed knelt down and stabbed himself in the abdomen. The other officer beheaded him too.

On November 26, 1970, the photo of Mishima's decapitated head was on front pages all over the globe.

In his biography, Nathan wrote about Mishima's grandmother, who isolated him for several years of his childhood, would not let him go out in the sun, and insisted that he play with dolls. She also had violent, morbid outbursts. Nathan also hints that the coup was only a cover for the dramatic suicide Mishima had dreamed of for years.

———

I enter the exhibit and walk down a series of dark halls that switch back and forth. But no matter where I turn in this labyrinth, inexplicably following me is a glowing sun, the symbol of Japan — of its past glory as the center of Asia, of how it conceived itself, and of how Mishima, after the war, continued to see it. *How can it possibly be following me?* I think as I make a sharp right, a fast left — but there it is over my shoulder.

The circuitous path leads to a large room, housing the frame of a disassembled house, hanging by wires from the ceiling. The door, a window frame, the siding, all dangling. It's Mishima's actual summer house blown open — not a duplicate, but the real thing transported here, with no foundation.

I come to a door. It appears to be an elevator. An attendant wearing short, white gloves asks me to wait for a few others to gather. Once they do, she gestures; the door opens wide. Only six of us are allowed in at a time.

We enter, and the heavy door is closed behind us.

I am with three Dutch and two English people, none from our tour group. I had become dislodged from our group as I stumbled, mesmerized, through the halls.

The cubicle is dark. We are not going up or down, as in a normal elevator. Spoken Japanese is being piped in — I presume they are Mishima's words. At the same time, through a projector, kanji letters are literally pouring over us and over all the walls. The voice gets more intense and the letters turn red. Mishima's words turn to blood as they continue to rain over us. We now are part of this installation, drenched in Mishima's self-destruction.

A door opens on the opposite side of where we entered. The other five people scurry away.

I drag myself out into a simple memorial at the end of

the exhibit. On a wall plaque is a long paragraph in English from Mishima, sounding a warning about industrialization, Japan's modernization, and the loss of the country's essence and soul.

I go through the exit. It is such a relief to be outside.

When I return to my room, I take out my notebook with lined paper — I brought no drawing pad — and ink in an image of the blue mountains as they come down to the inland sea outside my window. It is the least I can do for the most beautiful place I've ever been.

I skip the group dinner, but later that night I run into Mitsue. "C'mon," I tell her. "I'll take you to the fancy hotel restaurant. Treat you to tea and dessert." She lights up.

When we get there, six of our group are sitting at a long table. This crew has been treating themselves to a straight whiskey each night. It's become their rallying point. We join them.

The waiter comes over. I tell him, "Two teas, and what do you have for dessert?"

The waiter is firm but polite. "Oh, madam, the kitchen is closed. But we can serve tea."

I look over at the other tables, where guests are still eating. "Oh, come on. Slip us some dessert. Something you don't have to cook."

Mitsue pales, her eyes opening wide. This is Japan. You do not contradict. Rules are followed. "That is impossible," the waiter says stiffly.

"Nothing's impossible." I point to Mitsue, who I can

see wants to crawl under the table. "This poor girl is hungry. Where's your manager? I'm sure he'll understand." I am friendly. This is not a threat.

He blanches. "I can take you to him."

"Great." I follow him. Mitsue trails far behind. She doesn't want to be implicated, but she has to see this.

The waiter finds the manager, and the Japanese language starts flying. Mitsue pales even more. I stand there, resolute and smiling. It's easy when you don't know what's being said.

"Yes, it can be done," the waiter says firmly. "Please go back to your table." He flings out his arm, indicating the direction.

"Can you make it three?" I ask. I want to surprise Que, a tall, lanky Zen student who is one of the drinkers. He is way too thin. I'd like to fatten him up a bit.

"*Hai*," the waiter says, which I know means yes.

We return to our table. Now the whiskey drinkers are intrigued.

"You're getting dessert? Impossible."

"Yes; you'll see," I say.

Mitsue and I sip our tea. She is still in shock. She knows what proprieties I have shattered.

When we are almost to the bottom of our cups, the waiter approaches with a plate in each hand and one on his right forearm. He places two in front of us — nougat with ice cream — and hesitates with the third.

I point to Que. "Que, you need to eat."

Embarrassed and touched, and being a good Zen student, he shares his dessert with his drinking buddies.

"You're so skinny," I tell him. "I wanted you to eat it on

your own. They give such small portions. Maybe we should order more." Everyone bursts out laughing.

I have to convince Mitsue that it's all okay, but in her secret life, I know she is delighted. It marks a map to her own freedom.

I sign the bill to charge it to my room. Fifty dollars for this performance.

We're traveling back to Kyoto. We've taken one ferry and are now waiting for a train. The young couple are at it again. One long tender kiss, arresting lip-on-lip action. This is a kiss that leaks last night's love, spreading it all over the morning. I am so happy they came along. What's better than a good, lingering canoodle?

The train slides in on time and we take our seats. A few more chapters, and I'm done with *The Old Capital* by Kawabata. He might have been Mishima's rival for the Nobel, but he also was Mishima's early mentor and was haunted by Mishima's suicide. Kawabata had nightmares for hundreds of nights afterward.

The first half of the novel is slow, not big on plot. A young adopted woman, Chieko, the only child of a good couple, decides to take a short trip in the country. Purely by accident she meets her twin, Naeko, whom she never knew existed. Chieko has had all the advantages of a good home and of being immersed in the culture of Kyoto, while her sister cuts down trees for a living.

Chieko returns to Kyoto but does not tell her parents

right away what she has discovered. In between there are a lot of Kyoto festivals, talk of beautiful kimonos, and two men who want to court Chieko.

In the haiku-like simplicity of the novel's prose, layers of meaning are subtly conveyed. All emotion is subdued. Much of it is over my head. But, as if by osmosis, something is received, then digested.

This is also how I learned Zen. Nothing was explained. The practice seemed foreign and strange. Still, we showed up, imitating the teacher's sitting, walking, and bowing, and the essence bled through.

The second half of the book is livelier; the strands of the story come together. The son of the kimono shop owner, who weaves beautiful kimonos, wants to marry Chieko but ends up proposing to Naeko. His proposal is supported by Chieko. The reader begins to feel a confusion of identity. Who is who?

The plot reminds me of the Japanese folktale about a young woman named Chen who runs away with her childhood sweetheart when her father insists that she marry someone else. Years later, married, with two children, and having lived away for a long time, she takes her family to visit her parents. Her husband goes first, to announce their arrival.

Chen's father is confused.

"What do you mean?" he asks the husband. "Chen has never left. She has been sick in bed all these years."

Healthy Chen then enters. She is taken by her father to meet sick Chen, and they merge into one.

Zen students are sometimes presented with this story and asked, *Who is the real Chen?*

Several times in the Kawabata novel, the father wants to visit some old camphor trees. They are important to him. Like taking comfort among the giant redwoods? Or how Southerners talk of their camellias, magnolias, dogwood? Maybe it's his longing to be present once again to something rooted and fragrant — when the camphor tree, native to Japan, flowers in spring, its scent fills the lungs. Its huge, twisted trunks reaffirm a steadiness in this fragile life.

I don't dare ask anyone on the trip about camphor trees. They would whip out their iPhones and Google it. I want to encounter one without so much information. I think of Basho: *If you want to learn about a tree, go to the tree. Let nothing stand between you.*

Will I know a camphor when I see one?

Two Autumns

Shiki is another major Japanese haiku writer Ginsberg entreated us to study. Unlike the other three writers, Shiki, born in 1867, lived two years into the twentieth century. He had a short but intense life.

> Cockscombs
> must be 14
> or 15

I first heard this haiku by Shiki at least twenty years ago. It caught me the way Basho's frog and the old pond did.

Shiki was an invalid with tuberculosis. At thirteen, when he coughed up blood for the first time, he took the pen name Shiki, which in Sino-Japanese is translated as "cuckoo," the bird that, according to legend, coughs blood as it sings. This was his only concession to his illness. He continued to lead an active life, with enough charisma to inspire and propel a literary movement, even while ailing. He died at age thirty-four. During the last five years of his life he was completely bedridden. He suffered from excruciating back pain, fevers, festering tubular boils, and, according to his own description, swollen ankles and legs, diarrhea, indigestion, flatulence, nosebleeds, eye pain, terrible headaches. He was only free from pain when he took morphine.

> When I try to stand
> the hinges of my back
> are bitterly cold

As a child, Shiki was an inarticulate speaker and a slower learner than his early classmates. But eventually he became a scholar of modern Japanese literature and language.

Shiki's mother and sister cared for him throughout his life. When they were interviewed years later, they clearly had no idea that he had developed into a haiku master, with many disciples. They remembered him only as skinny, weak, ill, fragile, funny-looking, and not that smart.

I have a photo of Shiki from his final years. He is sitting on the edge of a tatami, gazing serenely out at a garden. At one point he wrote that "the little garden is my universe and its plants and flowers have become the sole material for my poems." They were like the water lilies to Monet in his late years. They were all he painted in his garden in Giverny when he was almost blind. And Georgia O'Keeffe, in her nineties, when she could no longer see well enough to read, had her young helper in the evenings read out loud the haiku from Blyth's haiku volumes.

Basho trekked in the wilderness to receive his haiku; Shiki sat alert at the edge of the garden.

Cockscombs
must be 14
or 15

I learned that cockscombs are those ruffled, velvety, convo-
luted flowers that grow in bunches and look like flames — or
like compacted, crested, plume-like heads. They can be yellow,
orange, or hot-red. I like to think Shiki's were red — the color
of lust, desire, blood. Close-up, the flower looks like brains.

So full of life in the middle of summer, those cockscombs
are contemplated by this very sick man, everything aching.
Vital flowers next to his diminishing body. One is growing;
one is wasting away.

But even in his suffering, he is able to ponder the cockscombs — how many, fourteen or fifteen? He accepts ambigu-
ity, a high mark for haiku. He accepts the mind of uncertainty
and expresses it, making this haiku modern: conversational,
banal, unassuming, mortal, almost like a whisper.

Shiki was alive at the very end of the nineteenth century,
when Japan moved out of the Tokugawa (or Edo) shogunate,
with its famous samurais, into the Meiji period. After centuries of insulation, the country was opening itself up to rapid
modernization.

Shiki was born into a samurai's family but cut his traditional long hair at the age of thirteen, marking his acceptance
of and entry into a new age. He rediscovered and resuscitated

haiku, as Basho and Buson had done before him. But Shiki broadened the idea of haiku. He had access to Western approaches to literature and painting and studied both deeply, using them to expand his haiku practice.

Before Shiki, haiku wasn't considered literature. Obviously Basho, Buson, and Issa deepened haiku, and it was used as an expression of an awake experience, like a Zen koan and a Way of practice, but often the masses yanked it back to the lighter side — to the first verse, a hokku, of a longer poem, a *renga*, composed by a social group at a party, a tea.

Shiki practiced haiku in new ways.

> Ocean and mountains
> way beyond
> seventeen syllables

He was born just as insular Japan was opened to the West and to radically new ideas and ways of seeing. For Shiki haiku was not only a way to express the changing reality of nature but also a way to express the poet's inner life simply and sincerely as an object of poetry.

> Cherries blooming
> people I remember
> all far away

Being an invalid, Shiki did not shy away from the pain of illness and those details. He used what was in his immediate field:

Talking to myself,
hugging a hot water bottle
gone tepid

As it spills over
In the autumn breeze, how red it looks
my tooth powder

Spring breezes —
How I'd love to throw a ball
Over a grassy field

Plum blossoms
one sprig
in my medicine bottle

Here are more of Shiki's haiku:

Spring departing —
no wife, no child
in this grass hut

Nearing death
even louder
autumn cicadas

Stifling heat —
tangled in confusion
I listen to thunder

And this one:

> Winter camellia
> using all its strength
> blooming red

You can feel how he is talking about himself in this last haiku, his huge effort to live and assert his vision through the camellia that pushes to bloom, even in cold, inclement weather.

Shiki loosened the old bonds of haiku in another way: he dared to break through Basho's deification and applied Western literary criticism to Basho's work. This was essential; without it, haiku never would have moved into the modern age.

Over the centuries, images that were fresh in Basho's time slowly became stale, then repeatedly overused, and eventually prescribed. Haiku writers would dutifully throw in a camellia, a butterfly, a cherry blossom. Haiku became like classical paintings. Natural objects became symbols rather than a howling red radish right in front of you.

While Shiki dismissed nine-tenths of Basho's poems, he also felt that the remaining tenth were enough to justify his high reputation, and said so publicly. This echoed what Basho himself said so long ago. *If you write ten, you are a master.*

> Anniversary of Basho
> alone
> I eat a persimmon

Shiki loved persimmons, which ripen in the fall. Basho died on October 12. This was Shiki's quiet celebration.

———————
———————

By criticizing Basho, Shiki pushed aside the mystical curtain, cracked the frozen focus on one idol, and was then able to discover Buson, who by then, more than a hundred years after his death, had become completely unknown as a haiku writer.

> In the summer rain
> the path
> has disappeared
> BUSON

For many decades before Shiki, Buson was recognized only as a painter. It is only because of Shiki that we also have Buson today.

Here are three more of Buson's haiku:

> The two plum trees —
> I love their blooming!
> One early, one later

> The rainy season
> and the river with no name
> a frightening thing

The high priest
relieved his noble bowels
in a desolate field

Then there is this one:

I go,
you stay;
two autumns

This haiku is attributed to Buson, but many scholars believe that Shiki wrote it.

I asked Kaz Tanahashi what he thought about this. He said, "Sounds like Shiki; could be Buson. Let's hang out in the mystery."

Shiki and his group of haiku poets observed the anniversary of Buson's death each year — just as Buson and his disciples remembered Basho's. But, because of his sickness, Shiki had to celebrate carefully and deliberately.

On September 18, 1902, Shiki was in unusually poor health. A close disciple, Hekigoto, was summoned to his bedside. When he arrived, a neighbor's wife and Shiki's sister Ritsu were sitting by his bed. His mother had gone to fetch medicine because his throat was so filled with phlegm that he couldn't even cough.

How much longer
is my life?
a brief night…

Ritsu prepared sumi ink by the sickbed. Shiki lay on his back; over his head, Ritsu held up his usual writing board; Hekigoto placed the writing brush in Shiki's hand.

Shiki slowly wrote out, word by word, three deathbed poems.

The first was his farewell to the world:

the gourd flowers bloom,
but look — here lies
phlegm-stuffed Buddha

The juice from gourds, gathered before they bloomed, was used to relieve his coughing. Now the juice was useless; so the flower was allowed to bloom as his death was blooming. Two opposites, held in the mind — and in the haiku. This is the haiku usually held up as his traditional death poem.

Then Shiki wrote two more:

a quart of phlegm —
even gourd water
couldn't mop it up

they didn't gather
gourd water
day before yesterday either

When you know the situation — his long sickness — these two final haiku come across as direct, blisteringly raw, a last cry. But they are still disciplined, still expressing the finality of what Shiki dealt with all his life. From the very beginning, Shiki knew he would die young, that many things would never be experienced.

A few hours later, he was dead.

Is there a single haiku of Shiki's that exemplifies his life? Perhaps this one:

> Autumn departs
> for me no gods
> no buddhas

A Fan

Sitting on a bus speeding toward Kyoto, I am staring out the window at the ever more urban scenery.

Joan plops down next to me. "Hey, I heard that Harada Roshi is coming to see you. He's terrific. A good friend of me and Kaz. He's eighty — very funny, wild." She imitates what he says: "'As we speak this very moment, all over Japan, Zen is fading away.' He's a stitch."

She can see by my face that I don't know what she's talking about.

"You don't know?" she says.

I shake my head.

"He's coming all the way from Takayama to meet you. Mitsue hasn't told you?"

Mitsue comes from the front of the bus with her iPhone in hand. "Harada-san wants us to meet him at the bus depot when he arrives."

I'm confused. I have no idea who this man is — and I'm hoping for a hot bath back at the Kyoto Hyatt. I tell her, "Have him meet us in the hotel lobby."

As Mitsue relays the message, I try to put the pieces

together. Is Harada the student she told me about on the bus to Osaka? The one who read *Writing Down the Bones* in Japanese?

"Who is he?" I ask Mitsue.

Joan moves to another seat. Mitsue sits down.

"He is a roshi from Takayama," she tells me. "He has a beautiful temple there."

"And he's eighty? Quick, call him back and tell him I can meet him at the bus station. I don't want him to have to do the extra traveling."

She shakes her head. Too late.

I'm toweling dry when the phone rings. "He's here." I hurry to dress in a black T-shirt and black pants. I notice that my hands are shaking.

I see Joan standing in the lobby near two white couches. A small wiry man in a black *hipari* stands behind her. He has his arms flung over Joan's shoulders. Joan is hunched over to assist, and both are wildly laughing, their mouths wide open. He seems to be attempting to jump on Joan's back.

I approach shyly.

Harada sees me and springs away. Everything slows down. He bows and then says in very broken English, "I am friend of Katagiri. He my big brother."

I do the math in my head. Roshi would have been eighty-six.

Harada says, "Ahead me in school. Eihei-ji together. Very serious, determined. He go to America, not known here in Japan. He bring Buddhism to America. Like Bodhidharma."

He then introduces me to a serious-looking man standing beside him. He is Harada's old student, Shinichi Ida, now a small publisher in Tokyo. He too has traveled here to meet me.

Harada's face is lit up, open, curious, straightforward. He reminds me a bit of Katagiri.

"Please," I say, "let's sit down. You've traveled a long way. We can order some food."

I grab Mitsue by the arm. I desperately need her to translate. I want very much to communicate with this man.

The four of us sit at a round table and order tea. Harada and Ida wave away the food menu.

We stare at each other in amazement. Harada cannot believe the author is here in the flesh. I had no idea this meeting was even going to happen.

Harada leans across the table and hands me something. "A present," he says.

It's a fan with calligraphy on it. And a card with an image of Ikkyu, a wild sixteenth-century poet and Zen master. On the back of the card is writing in blue ink: *The character of this fan was written by my friend Akiyo Sugano. It is song of Buson. Thank you I glad you came. Doichi Harada.*

"You write English very well." I bow my head, putting the fan to my forehead. I am embarrassed that I don't speak even a few words of Japanese.

Through Mitsue he asks me, "Did you teach high school?"

"Yes." I tell him. "Long ago."

I learn that, before he became a monk, Harada was a public school teacher, and Shinichi Ida was one of his students. They have continued to be friends. Then he tells me that he is writing a book. Denshobou, Ida's press, will publish it.

Both men pull out their copies of *Writing Down the Bones* in Japanese. Ida's copy has many yellow tabs.

"You have caught Katagiri's teachings," Harada says.

Ida leans over his notes. "How did you become spontaneous?" This seems to be a searching, personal question for Ida.

I've never been asked anything like that before. It is also a question I have never asked myself. To my American mind, the question itself is an obvious contradiction.

I throw up my hands and tell him, "From being Jewish." I'm half joking and half serious. I add, "Katagiri too was spontaneous."

Harada hits the heel of his hand playfully on his head. "I tell him he not free." This he pronounces without translation and pokes at Ida's side.

The waitress comes back. "Do you want anything else?"

I shake my head.

"What is United States? I hear 280 Zen priests there." He tilts his head as Mitsue translates my answer. He adds: "Doesn't matter. Only important one to one with teacher." All of Katagiri's students had that opportunity for intimacy with him but had to show up for it. That was the trick, showing up, not easy at 5:00 AM every morning. His consistency is what planted such a deep commitment in many of us.

Ida asks another question. It's about something I wrote in *Bones*.

I say, "Can you find the passage? I'm not sure. I wrote this book more than twenty-five years ago."

He bends over *Bones*, shuffling pages, but cannot find it.

I turn to Harada. "I wish you could read my other books, but they aren't in Japanese. Each one is influenced by my connection with Katagiri."

He says, "Students come. Some seem so hopeful. I get excited and then they leave."

I nod and tell him, "If you saw me during the first six years I studied with Katagiri, you'd never think I could have written this book. I didn't know what he was talking about."

Harada says, "I told Shinichi, 'Now, don't expect too much. Natalie has been traveling a long way and is tired.' But you have given us so much."

"Mitsue, tell Harada-san that meeting him has been worth my whole trip."

She tells him and he drops his head in a modest, pleased pose. "I can see why you and Katagiri got along. I've been watching you. Your wisdom doesn't come from your head but your whole body. That's how he was."

Harada says, "We would ask you to dinner —"

Mitsue shakes her head no. I can see how tired she is. It has been a very long day.

I say no as well. Without Mitsue we can't talk to each other. Plus, I need time to take this all in.

As we stand up, he repeats three times — and here his English is perfectly clear — "Katagiri was very lucky to meet you. Katagiri was very lucky to meet you." Each time he nods his head. "Katagiri was very lucky to meet you."

At breakfast the next morning, I ask Mitsue, "Why didn't you explain more about Harada-san when you picked me up at the airport in Osaka? I thought it was some high school or college writing student. I almost said no."

"I see." She laughs. "I could have told you more."

I ask her how she met Harada.

She nods. "A month before you arrived, I was escorting a friend of Kaz's to some of the Japanese sites. Kaz had told her about Enku, a wandering Buddhist monk and also a sculptor, who lived in the seventeenth century. Enku vowed to make two hundred thousand statues of Buddha. He would work quickly with only one tool. These wooden Buddhas are simple but very expressive. Kaz's friend wanted to see them.

"So we traveled to the Hida Mountains, where lots of these images were placed at Senko-ji Temple. We stayed at a ryokan in nearby Takayama.

"In the morning, when the innkeeper heard I was a Zen student in the US, he suggested I visit Shoso-ji Temple just a bit away. He told me that sometimes American students come, that the abbot is open-minded.

"I walked over to sit zazen there the next morning. I went early, but now the old abbot had retired. His son was the new abbot, and he was not happy to see me. He was busy getting his children off to school, I think.

"I left. Then, in the distance, about a hundred meters away, I saw a small monk down the road. He bowed to me out of the morning mist. We walked to each other and said hello.

Then he invited me to tea. When he found out I'd been living in the States, he asked, 'Do you know Natalie Goldberg? I'm looking for her.'

"I was shocked and suspicious. At first I didn't say anything. I didn't know who he was. But as we talked, I realized that he was the retired abbot of the temple.

"Then I told him, 'As a matter of fact, she's coming in three weeks. I'm meeting her at the airport.'"

As we sit there, I ask Mitsue about the structure of the Japanese language. I know that this is somehow connected to why she told me so little at first.

She pauses a long time, thinking. Then she says, "English builds from the inside out. Japanese from the outside in. The inside of Japanese is hollow, soft, empty of a personal self. You don't have to say everything. It can be ambiguous. Less is better. Least is best." She pauses again. "*Jibun* equals 'self.' Sometimes Japanese uses *I*, but not the concept of *I*. We think of another person and almost enter the other person's consciousness. We try to stand with the other's point of view. In the Japanese language we can even change what we are saying right in the middle if we see evidence that the other person doesn't like or agree with us. We want harmony. That is what matters."

She pauses once again. "This way of being sometimes brings problems. You care for a person, but your efforts to please are based on an assumption of the other person's needs and desires, and you could be wrong. Some Japanese do it in a very elegant way; they pave the road they believe you want to walk. But sometimes you don't want that road. People try to take care of you before you ask, and there is so much assumption. If the two people are Japanese, it works because they are both making an effort to arrive at the center between them, but with Americans I think the dialogue happens differently."

She rubs the edge of the table with her right hand, then reaches for tea. "It's why, I think, I left Japan for so long. I was exhausted from trying to second-guess everyone."

What You Want to See

The day before we leave Japan, I head out to find Buson's grave. This is not like visiting the Imperial Castle or a famous landmark. It's in a quiet, remote temple at the edge of Kyoto.

I ask directions from the concierge at the Hyatt, who writes and speaks passable English. Her answer is clear enough, but I can't keep track of all the details.

I hand her my notebook. "Please write down which bus, when, and what corner."

"*Hai.*" She writes for a minute and hands the notebook back to me.

I dart out the lobby door and walk to the distant bus stop. I wait fifteen minutes until the bus arrives. As I get on, I hand the bus driver my written directions. He nods and smiles. I have an uneasy feeling that this does not mean anything.

I sit behind the driver; we pull away. In a few minutes, the Hyatt — my one and only landmark — is gone.

Are we even going in the right direction? After twenty minutes I thrust the open notebook in the driver's face again.

He smiles and nods again.

I understand what this means: I am already lost.

I jump off at the next stop. Thousands of wires hum overhead. What do I do next? People in dark clothes walk by briskly. Low buildings with no signs run along both sides of the street. Dark clouds churn above. Slow drops of rain dot the sidewalk.

I see a cab — at least I think it's one. An old New York instinct makes me shoot out my hand. The car pulls over in front of me.

The rear passenger door opens automatically; the cab-driver is wearing white gloves. I lean over from the back seat and show him the directions. He grimaces and shakes his head. I try with my most Japanese accent: "Kompuku-ji. Buson. Mount Hiei." Naming the mountain rings a bell. The driver's expression changes and we head out.

The cab weaves from one street to another. At the base of one of Mount Hiei's foothills there are fewer people and less traffic. We turn a corner and head up a hill. Facing us is a high wall with bright-red Japanese maples peeking over. Then there is an open temple gate.

I am excited. The cabdriver is excited too that he found the temple. I give him a handful of bills and dash out.

Then I stop. This is a big moment. I try to compose my-self. This is why I came to Japan. I close my eyes.

I have made it here. I will meet Buson. I will thank him for that haiku I read so long ago, and for continuing Basho's lineage in his unique way.

I climb the stone steps up to the admission booth. I hand some yen to a stern woman with graying hair. She hands me a ticket and a large sheet of paper with a brief explanation in

English and photos at the bottom: Basho's hut, the tomb of Buson, and a drawing of Buson's.

I step into a side room, where I take off my shoes and gaze at an old Japanese painting of a lake with an aged man rowing a boat. No explanation. Next to it is a line of small paintings that seem to have something to do with Basho. I take my time, trying to absorb what I don't understand. I recognize a replica of a portrait of Basho, painted by Buson.

I put on my shoes and leave.

Farther up the steps, to the right of the temple, is a walking path. It leads me through a formal raked gravel garden, past meticulously hedged evergreens. From it, I see a layered reed roof: Basho's hut, the one Buson restored with his friends.

I hurry over. A window is propped open with a pole. I peek into the small, empty space. The wall is plastered a pale yellow. I try to imagine Basho here. Then Buson and his group of friends, drinking sake, writing haiku. Then Basho again, going on his long walks, partly to escape human distractions and the demands of society. Yet everywhere he wandered, he was known, often attracting attention and invitations he did not turn away.

I sit down on the veranda, under the thatched roof, protected from the drizzling rain. I let this, being here right now, be everything.

An old man and woman trudge up the path, peer into the window of the hut, and speak to each other. I smile; they ignore me, and the old loneliness fills me, but even that loneliness I let be.

I notice a plaque and then some stones with inscriptions — all in Japanese. I badly want to know what they say.

I step past formality and motion for the couple to come over. I point to the plaque. The man leans over the lettering for a long moment, then shakes his head. "Old," he says in English. I understand. It's old Japanese from another time, like Chaucer's English.

The couple wanders away. I see a wide footpath with moss-strewn stone steps heading up above the hut. I'm pretty sure it leads to Buson's grave.

I step slowly past shrubs thick with moss, ferns, pampas grass. I almost slip on knobby roots of thick trees jutting out on the path, glossed with rain. I stop. *Camphor trees?* — from Kawabata's novel. I look up. A flock of birds rises up around me, screeching.

> Camphor tree roots
> silently becoming wet
> in a winter shower
> BUSON

The path curves; I see gravestones ahead. I turn my head. More graves in crooks of the wet hill. All markers are rough-cut gray stone. What if I can't find his?

A little higher up is a cluster of stones; one seems more prominent. Could it be? I look down at the handout; Buson's engraved kanji on the tombstone is clearly visible. I look up, check, look down, look up. Match it. Yes. This is it. Here he is.

I put down everything I'm carrying — notebook, handout, purse.

I prostrate three times before the grave. The scattered

leaves and needles strewn on the ground smell rich and musky as I lower my head to the dirt.

> Autumn night
> it feels lonelier
> than last year
> BUSON

I stand up, suddenly shy. "What can I say?" I tell Buson. "Your haiku have touched me, centuries later, in another country. Thank you." I fold my hands over my chest, do a standing bow.

I leave the temple grounds, past those blazing maples, and wander — a bit dazed — through the narrow streets.

Four streets over, I follow the arrow on a sign and discover a shrine. It is on the spot where Miyamoto Musashi, the great swordsman, prayed before he single-handedly fought off an entire school of swordsmen who had challenged him. Because Musashi was famous and undefeated, he was constantly being provoked.

His unconventional two-handed method stymied his opponents. Often he came late, which unnerved their sense of decorum. Rather than studying with sword masters, he sought out the wisdom of Zen teachers, once walking a hundred miles to find one particular Zen monk hidden in the mountains.

Back at the Hyatt, I peel off my damp clothes and lie down on the bed with the one book I lugged from home: *Haiku Master Buson*, translated by Yuki Sawa and Edith Marcombe Shiffert. As I page through his haiku, tears come to my eyes.

> I grasp
> in the darkness of the heart
> a firefly

> A bad-tempered priest
> spilling from the bag as he walks
> the rice donations

> An evening shower!
> Holding onto the bushes
> a flock of sparrows

> They look beautiful
> after the autumn storm,
> the red peppers

> Morning glories —
> the indigo color on the towel's edge
> no longer satisfies me

> River in winter —
> who left behind on the bank
> a red turnip?

How visual his work is! All his years of painting served him well for writing haiku.

I turn the page.

> Going off to sleep,
> I want to hide in myself —
> winter isolation

So intimate, so close, he seems to expose himself more in haiku than did Basho, the stern one, his master, whom he never met.

Then I find my favorite of his haiku:

> While feeling sad —
> a fishing line being blown
> by the autumn wind

I remember reading a different translation, by R. H. Blyth, that begins, *Ah, grief and sadness!* I read that translation to Kaz and he squinched up his face. "That's too sentimental." I wonder if he'd like this translation of "feeling sad"?

More of Buson:

> *For the Death Anniversary of Basho*
> With the soundlessness of winter rain
> on mosses, vanished days
> are remembered.

Following the Master's Poem
The old pond's
frog is becoming aged
in the fallen leaves

Student to teacher, alive or dead, how the invisible web is woven and continues — and doesn't. You are on your own:

No trail to follow
where the teacher has wandered off —
the end of autumn

I page through more of the book. I start to read an essay Buson wrote about a man named Shoha, who had questioned him about haiku:

One day he questioned me again.

"Since old times there have been many different gateways to *haiku* and each is different. Which gateway shall I enter to reach the pavilion's innermost room?"

"There is only the haiku gateway itself. Think for yourself about what you have inside yourself. There is no other way. But still, if you don't choose appropriate friends to communicate with, it is difficult to reach that world."

Shoha asked, "Who are the friends?"

I answered, "Call on Kikaku, visit Ransetsu, recite with Sodo, accompany Onitsura."

I sit up in bed. All the haiku poets he names were connected with Basho — and even back then, all were dead. Buson is asking Shoha to reach beyond life and death.

Day after day you should meet these four old poets and get away from the distracting atmosphere of the cities. Wander around forests and drink and talk in the mountains. *It is best if you acquire haiku naturally.* Thus should you spend every day and some day you will meet the four poets again. Your appreciation of nature will be unchanged. Then you will close your eyes and seek for words. When you get haiku, you will open your eyes. Suddenly the four poets will have disappeared. You stand there alone in an ecstasy. At that time, flower fragrance comes with the wind and moon-light hovers on the water. This is the world of haiku.

Shoha smiled.

I leap up and grab the handout from the temple. I look at it more carefully. Those markers I wondered about — the ones on the slope, surrounding Buson's tomb — they are the graves of his disciples, his haiku friends and students.

Haiku writing is a true lineage.

Our final dinner is in a private room downstairs at the Hyatt. Still clutching the book on Buson, I sit next to Joan and whisper, "I want to share something with everyone."

Joan inclines her head. It's obvious how excited I am. "What's happened to you?" She hits a fork against an empty glass. Everyone quiets.

I stand up. "I made it to Buson's grave. Buson, the great haiku writer who came after Basho. I want to read you something he wrote."

I open up the book and read aloud:

"What you want to acquire, you should dare to acquire by any means. What you want to see, even though it is with difficulty, you should see. You should not let it pass, thinking there will be another chance to see it or to acquire it. It is quite unusual to have a second chance to materialize your desire."

I pause. My fellow travelers motion for more.

I read:

A winter night!
The old image of the Buddha
should be the first thing burned

The kissing redhead puts her hand to her mouth and chuckles. Que throws back his head and roars. Mitsue's face is full of pleasure. And the woman with the cast and crutches, who gallantly hobbled through our trip, seems the happiest of all. For the past two weeks, she has done what Buson advised: "What you want to see, even though it is with difficulty, you should see."

A Very Tender Way

Harada Roshi and I email each other for months after I return home. We send our messages through Mitsue, who kindly translates, and then sends on the translations to each of us. Harada-san often signs off: *I truly look forward to seeing you again. May you be content every day of your life.*

He tells me about his book, to be published by his old student, Ida. It will be called *Every Meeting Is Meeting My Life*, and he asks permission to include in it a section about our meeting in Kyoto. Of course I say yes.

As clarifications for his book, and as a way to deepen his understanding of Zen in America, he sends me questions to answer. The first one is, *What does Katagiri Roshi mean to you, as a human being and as a teacher?* He tells me that he plans for one of his book chapters to be about his old friend.

I respond:

I found in Katagiri someone who was very alive, very determined, very dedicated, very funny — he had a great sense of humor and was so sincere. He sat at 5:00 AM every morning, whether anyone showed up to sit with him or not. He used to say, "I don't sit for Minnesota Zen Center, I sit for all sentient beings forever." He was also very available to go and talk to. And I felt that he saw and understood my deepest self beyond my upbringing and conditioning. I felt safe enough to completely open my heart and in doing that I experienced a huge love I never thought possible. He also understood my love of writing and art and encouraged it. I call him "my great writing teacher."

Then, after taking a deep breath, I write a second paragraph, trying to keep it simple so Mitsue can translate:

In 1992 I wrote *Long Quiet Highway*, a glowing memoir about my studying with him. Six years after he died it was revealed that he had been sleeping with some of his female students. I was crushed and eventually wrote *The Great Failure*. I went back to Minnesota many times and did interviews and research. I spent two years writing the book. I wanted to understand what happened. I didn't blame him. I wanted to understand why I had been so naive. We understood so little about Zen and I think we all idealized him — he came from a foreign world. We put him on a pedestal. I think he was very lonely and he had no peers around him or support. Minnesota is a very cold place and when he lived there most people were white. He was very isolated and women were in love with him. I loved him enough to try to understand,

and in writing the book I grew up and became my own authority. But when I published it the sangha in Minnesota were angry even though they too had found out about these secrets. It was a very hard time for me. The book was published by a very good press and they had lawyers check on everything I wrote to make sure it was correct. I loved him too much not to try to understand his full dimensions. Also it made him more human.

I hesitate for a moment, then press Send.

Mitsue senses the importance of this particular exchange. I write it early on December 21, 2013; she translates it the same day and sends it on.

Before the day is over, I receive a translated response, sent to me with Mitsue's own personal note: "He is very thankful and continues to be delighted about this connection."

It is particularly cold in Santa Fe; earlier, snow had fallen. I open the attachment and read:

Words cannot express how much I appreciate your reply, especially your clear, direct answers. I wish I could read right away *The Great Failure*...It is not only in US that people put "roshi" on a pedestal. The image of it becomes so bigger than the real person. I need to pay attention to this matter myself (not to be treated as a senior teacher who accomplished more than he actually is??) while living, aging and dying.

It applies to all of us, living beings.

I also received an important message about relationships between teacher and his/her students.

I felt that you understood Katagiri's loneliness in a very tender way…

Anyway, the most important thing is to live yourself, wherever you are.

I WANTED TO GIVE A BIG THANK YOU TO THE UNIVERSE FOR THIS WONDERFUL MEETING.

In January and February, much snow falls in Takayama. Harada slips during one of his vigorous early morning walks and hurts his chest.

While he recovers in bed, he works on his book. He sends me a photo of a celebration in the zendo, accompanied by a painting of Buddha entering nirvana. He also sends me another photo: of *dango*, a treat like mochi, made from rice powder that is thrown in the snow and then retrieved.

He writes me, echoing Shiki:

I am getting old. I got injured. I have to be more careful, but the view from my bed is beautiful.

The Way of Haiku

The summer before I leave for Japan, I write this haiku:

> This black pen
> feels meaty
> in a writer's hand

Please don't imagine that my decades of writing practice and Zen meditation have silenced or fully pacified the angry self-critics in my head. That's not how things work. I'm just much better at managing those voices. After I write that haiku, my inner critic rises up and skewers me: *What does a black pen have to do with this beautiful July day? Meaty? Give me a break. You think you're a writer? Since when?* Next it goes for the jugular, unadorned and raw. It leaps: *I hate you; you're stupid.*

I'm at Vallecitos Mountain Retreat Center, a place I love. The sky is big; dragonflies flutter over the clear pool. I see the head of a beaver jutting out of the water on the far side. My legs are burning in the intense sun.

In that exquisite moment I let the critical voices pass. *It's okay*, I tell myself. *Try another.* I do:

on my brown socks
a single black butterfly
flaps its wings

Don't know where I'm going. But, okay, another:

a fire burns
across the valley
I want to go home

and another:

diving into
this ice-cold pond
my seventieth summer

I stand up on the deck, yank off my shirt and shorts, and do what I just wrote: enter the dark, frigid mountain lake fed by melting snow. I swim back and forth, gasping, panting, until I think, *Nat, if you don't stop now, you're going to die.*

I pull myself out, every pore alive. I think, *But haiku are not so dramatic. They're ordinary, subtle. I'm a bear grasping after a flower petal.*

I look around, towel wrapped across my belly, hair dripping. I can't take a step without stepping on a haiku. All around me, they're waiting.

full moon
behind clouds
your lips on mine

For years I believed in Ginsberg's idea that "the little sensation of space, nothing less than God" is the only true haiku test. But what if God exists quietly, without sensation or without space? What if God takes many different forms?

Plus, the idea of a haiku leap becomes too materialistic, creates grasping in the writer — me — and in the reader. It's easy to place too much value on that leap, to want something beyond what is. Trying too hard can kill the soul of what's being written. A haiku is bigger than one thing; I tell myself, *Don't try to contain it.* Yet, there is structure — three short lines. And within those lines there are multiple layers of resonances. Like the Basho frog haiku — it's taken me years to feel its luminosity.

Some people argue that a haiku written in English should cleave to five, seven, five syllables; some say it should always refer to a season. Structure is good, important; but in this moment, I utter, *Nah,* as I yank on my pants and reach through the sleeves of my cotton shirt.

Sitting again on the ratty, half-collapsed, outdoor chair at the pond, I think, *I've held myself hostage with Ginsberg's ideas since 1976.* What did Basho write for a student months before his death?

> Don't imitate me;
> it's as boring
> as two halves of a melon

When I arrive home from the retreat, I run my finger along the spines in my bookcase. I have a vague memory that, years ago, right before I left for Japan for the first time in 1998, I bought a book called *Chiyo-ni: Woman Haiku Master*, edited by Patricia Donegan and Yoshie Ishibashi. But I dashed off on my travels and never read it.

I open it now and see that the two editors signed it and even added an inscription: "For Natalie. In appreciation of a fellow writer." I turn the page, read further: "Chiyo-ni was born in 1703, seven years after Basho's death. For decades she was considered equal to and the counterpart of Basho. More importantly, she was known and respected because she lived the Way of Haiku: aware and open to every moment."

She was born in the small town of Matto, far in the north, with harsh winters that attuned her to seasonal changes. A Buddhist temple was nearby, with the ringing bells always in her ears. She wrote her first haiku at six and seven years old. Stopping in the midst of play in a rice field, she gazed up at the birds in the autumn sky:

> the first wild geese
> coming
> still coming

She was recognized for her early talent, and she had the opportunity to study with haiku masters. One of them, Shiko, stayed the night at her house, and in the morning he asked her to write a haiku on the iris:

> Spring
> remains
> in the iris

Shiko also wrote one for Chiyo-ni as he looked at the flower arrangement in the family alcove:

> no regret
> to use the hibiscus's shadow
> as a rain shelter

Though Shiko and Chiyo-ni met only that one time, they wrote letters to each other. She often asked him to comment on and improve her haiku. When he died, she wrote:

> sad, so sad
> to miss the plum flower
> before it fell

She became famous for her haiku — and her beauty. Yet Buson, who began the Basho revival during Chiyo-ni's lifetime, denied her, calling her work "woman's haiku, weak and emotional."

Eventually, though, Buson couldn't ignore her. He even asked her to write the introduction to his poetry collection, which was a great honor.

It is not clear that Chiyo-ni ever married, though some of her haiku show experience with romance and sensuality:

> what shadow
> can the star lovers meet in
> before the moon disappears

till his hat
fades into a butterfly
I yearned for him

woman's desire
deeply rooted —
the wild violets

eventually
whose skin will they touch —
rouge flowers

change of kimono:
showing only her back
to the blossom's fragrance

She continued to study with other haiku masters. Though she was well-known, she stayed humble, often asking younger poets, even twenty years younger, for their critiques.

At one meeting of haiku poets in Kyoto, where she was the only woman in attendance, she surprised everyone by writing the best haiku about the full moon — conveying the impression of a full moon without mentioning it:

this evening!
since the crescent moon
I've been waiting

When she was in her thirties, a succession of tragedies wiped out her family, leaving her alone to manage their scroll-making business. Because of this, she couldn't fully devote herself to writing haiku again until she was fifty.

At fifty-two she became a nun, but she did not live in a temple, as conventional nuns did. She lived at home but with the status of a nun, which gave her a certain freedom — and the rare privilege as a single woman to travel, meet male poets, and not be restricted by the normal social codes imposed on women.

She wrote her best haiku during this time. She wrote with prostitutes; created collaborative art with samurai; and wrote haiku as gifts for foreign visitors. Much of her work celebrates everyday life outside the temple — yet she never lost sight of what is sometimes called *sad beauty*: the understanding and acceptance of impermanence, that everything is transient.

> clear water:
> no front
> no back

> anyway
> leave it to the wind —
> pampas grass

She often painted illustrations of her haiku on the same sheets of paper, in a practice known as *haiga*, or haiku painting. In addition, she painted portraits, including one of Chigetsu, the most prominent woman disciple of Basho and a *haijin* — a master haiku poet living the Way of haiku.

Book in hand, I lower myself into the old oak rocker I bought many years ago. Why hadn't I ever heard of Chigetsu? Basho broke the old paradigm and created a Way, a practice, so he should be recognized. But there were women practicing that Way too. Until I encountered Donegan and Ishibashi's book, no whiff of that practice had ever passed through most of the books I read.

Four women poets were especially close to Chiyo-ni: Kasenjo, Shisenjo, Suejo, and Karyo-ni. Suejo was Chiyo-ni's main disciple and closest companion.

As she grew older, Chiyo-ni's health suffered:

> my energy
> can only defeat a butterfly
> this spring morning

She left behind several death poems, including these:

> clear water is cool
> fireflies vanish —
> there's nothing more

> I also saw the moon
> as for this world —
> ah — good-bye

When she died at seventy-two, she, like Basho and Buson, was surrounded by her close haiku friends and disciples, especially Suejo.

I knew when I listened to Ginsberg, so many years ago, that women were involved but not mentioned. I am not a patient person, but in this one way I am — I listen to the boys and wait with certainty that the women will be revealed. They have to — they were there too.

More by Chiyo-ni:

> morning glory —
> the truth is
> the flower hates people

> moonlit night —
> a cricket sings
> out on a stone

When I talk with Mitsue on the phone and tell her I found this woman haiku writer, she says, "I think we studied Chiyo-ni in school, but no one said she was a woman."

> she also cups
> the spring water
> for her travel writing brush

> twilight
> is left
> in the maple leaves

> unfinished dream —
> a chrysanthemum blooms
> in the tatami room

The Fall

It's October 2016. In ten days I will fly back to Japan. It has been four years. During that time I've had cancer and recovered. Harada is now eighty-three. I feel the pressure of time.

On this trip, I will not go with a group. Instead, I have contacted Alastair, a longtime writing/Zen student who speaks passable Japanese and who has led groups to Japan eight times. I told him that Armely, another writing/Zen student, and I wanted to go to Japan and follow Basho's path — what we can of it. Did he want to help us plan and come along? All three of us will practice as we go: meditate on cold cement benches in train stations; do writing practice on the long rides from one destination to another; have periods of silence as we walk. We want to spend the entire month of November in Japan. After some negotiation, emails flying back and forth, Alastair agreed to be our translator, private tour guide, and co-practitioner.

Alastair suggested different itineraries, then changed his mind about them. "As long as we go to Matsushima," I told him, "I'm open to any plans."

One of Basho's most famous haiku is about the place:

Matsushima ah
Matsushima ah
ah, Matsushima

Now, ten days before I fly to Tokyo, I recite this haiku again. I imagine Matsushima as a great and beautiful mountain, and I want to see it for myself.

On the afternoon before Yom Kippur, I'm driving home from an appointment. In a few hours, as the sun sets, I'll be in the synagogue — the one time each year I attend. I go to beckon in the Day of Atonement, the holiest day of all in Judaism, with a prayer shawl around my shoulders. I always heed this day, feel its power, never deny my heritage.

I'm driving north through Santa Fe on Guadalupe, the military cemetery on my right, a car going in the same direction on my left. I don't see the beige Buick dart perpendicular across three lanes, aiming for the cemetery entrance. In the front seat, a couple in their late seventies, maybe eighties. No time to brake.

I smack head-on into their passenger side. My airbags blow open. The front of my car looks like an accordion.

I jump out, afraid my car will explode, and run across to the Buick.

Both people's heads are bowed; their bodies hang forward from their seat belts. Dead? Unconscious?

I fall back on the grass, shattered glass on my shirt, a big gash on my knee, cuts on my hands. No bones broken.

Eventually the police arrive. Both people in the Buick wake up. Witnesses tell the police it is the couple's fault. An ambulance comes and takes the now-conscious couple away. Soon I am alone in the back of another ambulance. The attendant tells me the couple was a brother and sister, going to their brother's funeral.

On the way to the hospital, I replay the events in my head. When my car struck the Buick, I had only one thought: *I am going to Japan.*

Back home a few hours later, bruised and battered but not seriously injured, and declared fit to travel by the emergency doctor, I go for broke and upgrade my plane reservation to business class.

———

Now I'm in Tokyo, in a tiny hotel room. It has a bed, a small desk six inches away, a teapot, bags of good green tea, and, amazingly, a set of pale-yellow cotton pajamas. I have arrived three days early to catch up with jet lag. Secretly I love jet lag. It's the only situation in which I sleep deeply, so I take advantage of it, milk it for all it's worth. I sleep and sleep.

Infinite Light

Alastair has figured out the way to Chuson-ji, a collection of temples deep in the mountains where Basho wrote an important haiku:

> The summer grass
> is all that's left
> of an ancient warrior's dream

So far, as much as possible, we have tried to walk to our destinations, after we have taken a train or bus to the general area.

Following in Basho's exact footsteps is impossible, of course. Many cities, towns, buildings, highways, walls, and fences have been constructed since he was trekking. The challenge has been to walk as much as we can, and to drop our minds down to a minimal level of thinking. We want to walk intimately with our surroundings, moment by moment.

Many nights the rain has been relentless on the eaves of the ryokans and small hotels we stay in, but today is warm and incandescent, a rogue summer day in the middle of

November. As we climb through the cryptomeria forest, a strange melancholy fills us. We know this is summer's last stand.

We pass a vegetable garden to one side of the road — tomatoes drooping on the vine, ruined by night cold. But bright-green leafy vegetables still stand proud. We wave to the elderly couple who are tending them.

A young, odd-looking man is walking in the other direction. As he nears us, Alastair asks him, in Japanese, if we are on the right path to Chuson-ji. He nods — and then he turns and follows us. We aren't sure if he wants to be helpful, is lonely, or plans to rob us.

We pass by one huge house after another, some behind concrete walls with tiled roofs peeking over. Then stone gardens, and low Japanese maples in pink and gold.

At a curve, the trail heads up the mountain, away from civilization. It grows steeper and steeper, leaving the last traces of summer below us.

My knees are sore and I'm slowing down. My body is coming out of the shock of the car accident. Alastair and Armely are ahead of me, but the young Japanese man — tawdry in brown pants, a rumpled yellow shirt, and oxfords — is directly behind me. I get a bit nervous, then remember: *It's Japan. There's so little crime here.*

We keep climbing — my calves are burning — and come to a raised wooden walkway and then occasional wooden bells, which I know are used to scare away bears. When I reach one, I ring it hard.

We keep walking in silence, hearing the creak of the wooden planks in each step. It's late and the air is cold. We are in ebony shadows that swallow up the giant cryptomerias. The walk ends in a wide path through groves of tall bamboo, which draw our gazes up to the entrance of Chuson-ji. It has appeared out of nowhere, at the top of Mount Kanzan.

We see a large, mostly empty parking lot, a ticket booth, and a few other tourists. Most of the day's visitors have already left. Dusk is deepening.

We enter the complex. Many of the ancient buildings have burned down and been rebuilt. But, over the centuries, Konjikido, the golden hall, has been preserved.

The hall is dedicated to the Buddha of Infinite Light, in a call for peace and mercy, a call for allies and rivals alike — even for birds and insects, everything that died in those terrible battles centuries ago — to find resolution, contentment, and comfort.

We approach Konjikido, passing other tourists who are on their way out. By the time we reach the entrance, night has fallen.

It's a small temple. Maybe the size of a bedroom. But as we step inside, we are filled with radiant light.

My mouth falls open. I have never seen anything like this — not in Kyoto, Nara, other Japanese locations, or any other place I have ever been.

The interior is entirely gold, with lacquer and mother-of-pearl inlays. Inside are thirty-two Buddhas of infinite light; bodhisattvas of compassion and wisdom; *Jizos*, protectors of women and children; and fierce guardians in poses I've seen at other temples' gates — all covered in gold leaf. The entire room is luminous.

Well-being pours through me, followed by this sentence:

I don't have to be afraid to die. If the human imagination could conceive of this room, raining light and love beyond any limits —

I got it all wrong. Life and death are limitless, far beyond what we can conceive. All at once, no birth or death — just this great golden song of light, resounding like a temple bell. This state beyond craving, fear, and ignorance.

Far-off bells ring, signaling the closing of the complex. We step outside under the ten thousand stars.

Armely and Alastair, walking ahead, turn around, smile, and tell me they're headed for the museum and gift shop. I say that I'll join them in a few minutes.

I wander in the dark among the other closed temples and outbuildings. People in groups pass me, laughing, heading away.

I see a dim statue in the distance and walk up to it. It's of Basho, in his sandals, a cap on his head, a cape over his shoulders, clutching a parcel to his chest. A walking stick in his hand, a round rain hat hung on his back. He is standing with feet apart, his expression attentive, perhaps forming a haiku in his mind, the one he wrote here at Chuson-ji:

> The summer grass
> is all that's left
> of an ancient warrior's dream

Six hundred years after Chuson-ji was built, Basho visited and wept, knowing his people's history and their suffering.

"Thank you," I whisper, "for bringing me here." I pause. "This is why I came to Japan."

Something Much Wilder

We are headed to Takayama, a town in the north of Japan, to meet with Harada Roshi at his and his son's temple.

We change trains in the city of Nagoya, where we are to meet Mitsue at the station. She is traveling from Naoshima, where she has been working as a photographer for the past three years. She will, once again, act as our translator with Harada. This meeting at the switching of trains has been planned by Alastair.

I spot her first. She is standing on the platform, holding a small black suitcase. I feel the strange joy of seeing someone after not seeing them for a bundle of years, as well as delight at how sophisticated she has become. Her hair is short on one side, long on the other, and she wears a perfect green draped blouse. We grab each other and hug tightly.

Minutes later, the train pulls in. The four of us climb aboard.

We have a long ride into the evening. Armely and Alastair begin to get acquainted with Mitsue, and Armely gives her a reading with Tarot cards. Mitsue pulls a two of pentacles.

"This card shows a person juggling two balls with a star in both hands," Armely explains. "When a person gets this card, it means she is confronted with choices." This opens up into a discussion of whether Mitsue will stay in Japan or return to the States.

I'm aware of how astounding this moment is. We are going back to where Mitsue first encountered Harada by accident, through enormous good luck.

I look at all three of my companions closely. Alastair's face is softening. I wonder if he is developing a crush on Mitsue. Armely is leaning over the cards, concentrating, a shadow of blue around her eyes. Mitsue keeps smiling.

Takayama is a mountain town with a mountain climate. Here we feel the close bite of winter. But it's still late autumn, with persimmons the color of apricots dangling from otherwise naked trees. We stay in the same ryokan where Mitsue stayed years ago, a short walk to Harada's temple.

The next morning, I wake early and step outside to see steep hillsides of trees changing colors. I carefully walk around a chained dog in the ryokan alcove. There is a chill in the air. I begin walking down the quiet lane.

In the distance, at a crossroad, Harada suddenly appears, a knit cap on his head. He turns and sees me, and his face lights up.

Soon we are face-to-face. We both throw out our arms in silence and smile. We hug briefly. Then he points down the road, as if to say, *I need to go now; I'll see you later.* I nod, and he leaves.

I keep walking down the lane under the early gray sky.

I pass tiled houses and deep-green gardens, plantings that thrive in colder weather.

A few minutes later, I see Armely up ahead. I whistle and she turns around and sees me. I motion for her to wait up. Dark-blue mountains surround us in the distance.

Soon we are walking together silently. I point out persimmons dangling from a tree and nod. *Go ahead.* I know that, before our trip ends, she is determined to pluck a ripe one directly from a branch and devour it. I nod again toward the tree.

She climbs up the slope beyond the front yard. She looks back at me; I lean back, look at the front of the house. I say in a loud whisper, "All clear."

She plants one foot on a high stone, her yellow tights exposed almost to her waist. Then she yanks down a full, heavy branch, stretching with her right arm for the deep-orange fruit, palming them for softness, finally plucking one off the branch. She hurries off the property and chomps into the stolen fruit. She turns and thanks the tree, and then its unseen owner.

As we walk back to the inn, I tell her how Shiki loved persimmons, and I recite this haiku to her from memory:

> Evening prayer bell —
> a ripe persimmon
> thumps to the ground

For years I'd seen the most beautiful Japanese drawings of persimmons before I even knew what they were. None of that fruit grew in Brooklyn, or New Mexico, or Minnesota. Then, when I was in my late forties, my sister sent me a box of them from Southern California. They were so lovely — the color so stunning — that I couldn't eat them. I lined them up on the windowsill and painted watercolors of them.

In midmorning, the four of us walk down to Harada's temple. On the left, we pass a long flight of stairs built into the hillside, leading to the local cemetery. I arch my head back to see how high up the stairs go. In one of his emails, Harada told me that he climbs them every morning, as part of his daily early-morning exercise. I can't see the top.

Taiseki, Harada's eldest son and now the abbot, greets us at the door to the temple.

Mitsue translates, "It's not used daily, mostly for special occasions, so it's not heated now. Please remove your shoes."

Mitsue turns her head and we follow with our eyes, looking where she is looking. Harada-san (I have now naturally begun to add the *san* to his name; it is a sign of affection and respect) has just entered the temple. My face lights up and I go to him. We give each other a long hug, then I take his hand. "I want you to meet my two students," and I lead him over to Armely. He nods, puts his hands together, and bows. I can feel the pleasure in this meeting. Armely is grinning ear to ear.

"And this is Alastair," I say. Recognition flushes over Harada-san's face as he looks up at this tall, blond man. Harada grabs him by the arm and takes him into the first room. All of us follow.

We stand before an elaborate gold altar with three tiers up to where three gold Buddhas reside. Above us is an elaborate wood ceiling. The walls are white, sectioned by dark wood. Fresh mums are in the two vases on a table before the altar, where a green incense bowl is in front of an unlit white candle. Porcelain statues in different colored robes are to the left of the gold altar.

We appropriately ooh and ahh, but already the bone cold that has built over weeks of no heat is seeping up through the polished dark wood floor and into my bare feet.

Harada-san points and explains altar details, and Mitsue gives short translations. We nod and follow him into the next area, full of upright statues. The atmosphere feels formal, and Alastair innocently asks in Japanese, "Which one is Ananda, Buddha's close companion?"

Suddenly, Harada and son start picking up statues, scrutinizing the bases to see if any has a name written underneath. This totally breaks the formality.

The son, who I was told could be unsociable and distant, stops in the middle of leaning back to see the bottom of one statue held high. He looks me up and down. Then he asks Mitsue — clearly his stiffness has relaxed — "What are these three Americans doing in Japan, anyway?"

"They are following in Basho's footsteps," she tells him.

He says something.

She turns to me. "Taiseki wants to hear a haiku. One of Basho's."

I nod, stand up tall, and recite — in English. I enunciate each word carefully, wanting to express my love and respect for Basho in this chilly echoing temple:

Sick on the journey
my dreams wander
over withered fields

This is Basho's death haiku. Mitsue translates as I tell the story behind it.

Basho had been on a pilgrimage, visiting the southern coast of Lake Biwa, when he became ill with a stomach ailment, so he detoured to nearby Osaka, to a friend's home. It was autumn, and he must have been aware of his approaching death. At his friend's house, he went to bed.

Many of Basho's disciples heard about Basho's illness, hurried to Osaka, and gathered at his bedside. He was calm as he wrote a note to his elder brother: "I am sorry to have to leave you now..."

According to a disciple's record, he thought only of poetry, day and night. Poetry became an obsession — "a sinful attachment," as Basho himself called it. Even when he should have been attending to his approaching death, he wrote haiku.

But maybe the disciple was wrong, I tell the group, or at least shortsighted. Maybe writing haiku was exactly the proper thing for Basho to do on his deathbed. I take out of my backpack the book I have about Buson and read what Buson said during his own final days: "Even being sick like this, my fondness for the way is beyond reason, and I try to make haiku. The heights of 'My dream hovers over withered fields' — Basho's last haiku — is impossible for me to reach. Therefore, the old poet Basho's greatness is supremely moving to me now."

I am slightly embarrassed by my enthusiasm, but the reason I am so up on this last Basho haiku is that I've been intensely studying it after reading Buson's comment. And yet, I don't quite get its greatness.

Immediately, a lively discussion flies back and forth across the altar room among Harada, Taiseki, and Mitsue.

After more than a minute, Mitsue turns to me and says, "It's not *withered fields*. Poor translation."

"No? What is it?"

They confer again for a long time.

It seems this is important to the three of them. Mitsue then explains, "Something much wilder. After everything has died and it's all removed — the stubble, everything — the fields are totally empty, truly vast."

I take a step back. Tears spring to my eyes. On his deathbed, Basho embraced the whole impermanent field of the universe.

Harada points out an old wooden statue — rough, raw, carved with not much of a face. A simple humility shines through. Harada explains, through Mitsue, that this is one of the sculptor Enku's oldest carvings.

In 1639, after losing his mother at age seven, Enku became a Buddhist monk. The temple he entered accepted many ways to realize enlightenment, including the way of the artist. That became Enku's way.

As an adult, Enku traveled around Japan, vowing to carve

two hundred thousand Buddha statues out of tree stumps or wood scraps — whatever he could find. He carved each one — no two alike — with a few strokes of a hatchet. Some were offered as comfort to the sick, others as reminders to guide the dying.

Harada tells us that Enku is the most famous of Japanese sculptors. In the afternoon, he promises, we will visit more temples with Enku's figures.

Harada then ushers us into a side room, where the five of us have tea, joined by Taiseki's wife, Yuko.

As we sip the tea, I present Harada with a bear fetish from Zuni, a pueblo southwest of Albuquerque. Through Mitsue, I explain that the bear is hand-carved turquoise, and that it symbolizes great strength, power, healing, and self-knowledge.

Harada's face lights up as he turns the figure in the palm of his hand. He pets the bear and nods to me.

I have also brought several small leather wallets as presents. Back in the States, friends have loved them. I offer one to Yuko. She shifts it around on the table, clearly confused. I realize then that Japanese purses are all made of beautiful cloth. To Yuko, what I have just given her is bland, maybe even crude. And I forgot to wrap it, a second mistake. In Japan, the pleasure of the gift lies as much in presentation — the wrapping — as what's inside.

Through the wood-grilled windows, I glance at yellow Japanese maples under a light-gray sky.

That night, back in the ryokan, making my way down the dark hall to the bathroom in the wee hours, I begin to re-think my mother's death. All the eight years after my father passed, my mother lived alone in Florida. If I ever broached the subject of death, she looked at me with her black eyes, the left one askew from a botched cataract surgery, and said, "You are so unkind and discourteous." I never had a hint what she thought about it, though late at night when I visited, I'd hear her, lying in bed, speaking to those who went before: her mother, her husband.

At ninety-two, in late December, she breathed heavily as I sat by her bed, "Natli, I'm dying."

I wasn't sure what to say. I took a shot, thinking of her late-night talks. "Are you going to see Grandma and Daddy?"

She jerked her head around. "You gotta be kidding. They dig a hole and put you in, and that's that." She closed her eyes.

After a pause, she opened her eyes again. "Buy me a little nicer coffin than you bought Daddy." His was simple pine.

"Yes, I'll do that," I promised.

That was it. In the last moment, right at the brink, no embellishment. My mother, almost a different woman. No comfort. No deliberation. She was much tougher than I ever imagined.

I realize, lying there in the ryokan, that my mother had her own great courage. Maybe her last pronouncements were too raw for me.

Basho's last haiku was mystical, poetic — he mentions his illness and in the same breath overcomes it in a dream, trusting a large imagination. But Shiki would have recognized and approved of my mother's death comments, grounded in an artless truth. He wrote:

> I turn my back
> on Buddha and face
> the cool moon

I hardly sleep the rest of the night but feel clear the next morning.

Wherever we go in Takayama, Harada drives us. On our first ride he tells us, throwing up his left hand, "There was an announcement on the radio this morning: 'Old people are a hazard and should not be driving.'" Then he swivels his head around and laughs.

I sit in the back with Armely. Even from behind I can see Harada's delight in driving. I watch his shaved head, with his big ears, the spotted blue skin of his neck jutting out from his wool cap, his pale wrinkled hands gripping the steering wheel.

On our third night in Takayama, Harada and Fumiko, his wife, take the three of us, plus his daughter Naoko and granddaughter Haruna, out to a very elegant dinner of endless courses in the back room of a restaurant. We sit on the floor, me between Alastair and Harada. We jab at conversation in slow English with Harada's moon-faced seventeen-year-old granddaughter, who sits opposite us. We speak about the intense exams she is studying for. I ask her if she can recite some of the haiku she learned in school. She blushes and shakes her head.

But then she says, "You know Trudeau from Canada? I like him." She adds, "He is honest, more simple."

Alastair, downing another cup of sake, says, "Handsome too. And young. He boxes."

Haruna is now enjoying the conversation, and her English suddenly improves.

I ask her if she's read Kenzaburo Oe, the Nobel Prize winner.

No.

Tanizaki?

She shakes her head and offers, "Have you seen Kurosawa?"

Alastair chimes in, "*Seven Samurai*? *Ran*?"

Naoko, Harada's daughter, tells us that her mother won third place in a newspaper haiku contest. I insist that Fumiko recite her haiku. Fumiko smiles and speaks; Mitsue translates:

> Sunset
> the frog with its short life
> singing for all it's worth

My mouth hangs open in delight. "Terrific," I say. And I mean it.

Fumiko bows her head, pleased.

Raw tuna with two small bright-green ginkgo nuts is placed before me. I mistake the nuts for grapes and pop them in my mouth. I am surprised by the texture, but like them.

Cold soba noodles, specially brought over from a neighboring valley, are served next.

There are many questions I want to ask Harada-san — about Zen, about my teacher Katagiri — but after all the time and effort it took to arrive at this moment, I feel inexplicably reticent. I speak a little, but mostly I eat. The language barrier is still hard. I do notice that, since our last visit, Harada-san has learned more English words.

After two hours, the final course is served. By now I have dropped any beginning or end. A single ball of vanilla ice cream drenched in plum brandy is placed before me, with an unrecognizable fruit on either side.

Half an hour later, Harada-san drops us off at our ryokan. We are all very full. We wave as he drives off into the night.

Mitsue and I stand together, gazing at the dark mountain shadows.

She says to me, "I tried to give you a chance earlier to speak privately with Harada-san. You were in the coffee shop with Alastair."

I think, *Why didn't you come in and get me?* I realize instantly that this is not the Japanese way. Too overt, too direct.

She explains, "We stood out near the street, across from the café from where you were. He talked with me about the book you wrote about his friend's failings."

"You mean my teacher? Katagiri?"

She nods. "He said in Buddhist or religious communities, people want to be close, tend to stick together for security. He said, 'I admire Natalie for her honesty. Someone has to be very rooted in Zen to do that, willing to break out of that circle.'"

In the ryokan's breakfast room the next morning, Fumiko and Harada-san join us, bearing gifts — scarves, a haiku scroll, calligraphy, a notebook — all impeccably wrapped in tissue paper. Above the door of the breakfast room hangs a wild, beautiful calligraphy of a famous children's poem Harada created years ago. I suspect it is hung here because he is prominent in the area, and beloved, and his temple is just down the road.

As we eat, Fumiko recites in a full voice a haiku she wrote earlier that morning, as snow whirled out her window. It is about longing and departure. It is in Japanese, of course. Mitsue translates. I no longer recall the exact words, but its intent — and its haunting sensibility — is clear.

Harada and his wife leave in a flurry of hugs and bows. We watch them disappear down the road as the snow falls. It lands on the pond near the door, on the sharp rocks, on the stunted branches of the two dwarf pines, and, vanishing, on the dark water.

> Morning chill
> I savor this moment —
> one meeting one lifetime
> FUMIKO HARADA

Wanting to See

In between my trips to Japan, I decide to make a concerted effort to write haiku. I hear about a Santa Fe haiku study group that meets at the local library the last Tuesday of every month. They don't count syllables. Just three short lines. Another group I hear about counts syllables and meets in an open field near my house, but with no regularity.

I think it's good to be aware of both: counting and not counting. If I didn't count a bit, rein in each line, I'd end up galloping into a short story. And if I only cared about syllables, I'd have a block of words with no soul.

Capturing the spirit of haiku is what I am most interested in. And haiku asks for a spirit that's not so human centered.

I drive to the library at the end of March. It's snowing out, the first and only snow we've had since autumn. But now it's spring and the apricot blossoms, always early, stunning in pale pink, will freeze. The roads are full of slow traffic. Santa Feans are fearful of both snow and rain, and even more of slush.

At the library, eleven people — eight women and three men — sit around three white tables pushed together. Some look familiar. One man, Charles Trumbull, I already know. He is very experienced in the haiku world, and he is giving us a lesson on Western elements of poetry — metaphor, simile, rhyme, personification, pathetic fallacy, and so on. I left these behind long ago in English classes.

All this is written on a handout. We turn the page over and Charles says: "*Wabi-sabi* is the Japanese aesthetics: asymmetrical, a sense of roughness, an intimacy, a closeness — it's different from Western concerns." Then he calls on a woman with a brown hat to read from the sheet: "Within the aesthetics is an awareness of the three marks of existence — what Buddhism teaches — impermanence, suffering, and egolessness, an absence of an individual nature."

I pay close attention. I'm pleased to hear the link between Zen and the essence of haiku. Then Charles also mentions simplicity, respect for natural integrity, and loneliness as a fundamental reality. He tells us the story of how Rikyu, the tea master, conducted a tea ceremony — "not a perfect cup, but one perhaps chipped, unbalanced, not round, so the imperfect truth can enter."

We were supposed to each bring in at least ten copies of one haiku to pass around. But first we go around the room and each of us reads aloud another one we have brought in. I have the one I wrote by the pond the previous summer:

> On my brown socks
> a single black butterfly
> flaps its wings

This round is a way to warm up. There are to be no comments. We move swiftly from one person to the next and the next, like popping corn. But even that quickly I can tell that people are at different levels of haiku experience. I surmise that this is a very democratic group.

When I read my brown socks haiku, it falls like a dead horse on dead ears.

I've had this experience many times before, but mostly when I read prose aloud. It's a great way to measure your work, even without a comment from the listeners. You can feel if your words physically connect to others. This process denotes whether your work is present, cuts through others' discursive thinking, and meets their minds.

Now each person takes a turn passing out a single haiku. Cynthia, the woman next to me, economizes and passes out her haiku on the tiniest pieces of paper.

The group comments about the paper size. Evidently, this is a running joke — indirectly it's also about the size of haiku.

Now we each have her haiku in front of us.

She reads it aloud twice:

> I see her smile
> In the sundrenched wild asters
> I smile back

A long pause and then the comments fly. Cynthia, the writer, nods and takes notes.

"You can take out 'I see,'" says the man opposite me.

"How about changing the first *smile* to *face*," says the

petite woman in a beige linen blouse. "You already have one *smile*. You don't need two."

"No, I like two smiles. It builds rhythm," says the man, who has been gone from the group for six months and just returned.

Then it is my turn. I pass out what now seems an enormous whole sheet of paper handprinted in big letters, with three haiku on it.

"Which one do you want us to look at?" asks Harriet.

I read it twice:

> Diving into
> this ice-cold pond
> My seventieth summer

"Go for it," I tell my fellow haiku writers. "I want to learn."

"Maybe glacier instead of ice-cold, to indicate high in the mountains?"

"Glacier has a slower sense, like being seventy — don't spell out the age. Keep it short," comments Sondra, the woman who sends out meeting announcements. She and Charles began the group five years ago. They met on Craigslist. Sondra put out a request for haiku writers, and Charles was the only one who initially responded.

"Maybe put 'my seventieth summer' first to give more punch, more distance between images," says a woman who drives up from Albuquerque each month.

I nod. I take notes, imitating the person before me.

I like this group. I also want to scream. But I decide to continue with the practice, to see where it leads.

I keep coming to the group. I never miss a meeting, month after month. And I keep writing haiku.

Eventually, what I begin to enjoy most is simply not knowing how to do it. I haul in my haiku each month, and they usually land like lead. I like not being good, not having a clue.

At the end of meetings, I'm sometimes pulled aside. Someone urges me, "Read a lot of them." Another suggests, "Write a lot of them." Exactly what I tell my own writing students about writing.

I walk to the library from my house. I go early, so I can stop at the cheese store on the way and sample bleu cheese.

We settle into our seats and go around, each reading a haiku like we do at the beginning of every session. It's deep summer now, and the air conditioning is on way too high. But Santa Fe has been unusually hot this June.

Sharon, sitting opposite me, reads:

> blackberry brambles
> along the road
> blues on the radio

Wow. Those *bs* and *rs* — I feel the roll and rhyme of it. And at the same time, the tangle, the jazz of it. Sharon flutters her paper in her hands, leans her elbows on the table. She has no idea how deeply I am affected.

Next is Charles, sitting in the corner. Charles has just lost a good haiku friend; he'd been at her bedside during her final days. He reads:

> hospice clock
> the shadow of the second hand
> catches up

He reads it again. I quietly gasp. *Oh my god, the dark reaper, even in the clock hand.*

I'm undone by two fine haiku in a row.

It's clear Charles doesn't know how good his haiku is. I tell him; Sondra agrees. "Gee, great," he says.

Sondra now hands out the smallest pieces of paper with three haiku on them and the heading: Santa Fe Haiku Study Group / June 26, 2018.

She reads twice the first one:

> a yelping dog
> drives the heat deeper
> summer night

I know exactly how she feels. Day after day, the heat has shot to the mid-90s, with little relief, even when the sun goes down. People jump in to comment. One person says, "How about taking out 'drives' and beginning the second line with 'deepens'?"

I like this haiku a lot and want to help. I look down at the paper and everything drops away. My concentration is intense. I can hear vague voices around me. I come up for air, as though I'd been underwater. "Sondra, how about 'the hot dog' —"

She hits my arm. "I don't want a hot dog in my haiku." Everyone bursts out laughing. I look around. I meant a heated animal. But I get it and laugh with them.

Now it's my turn:

> *Early Spring*
> I will not budge
> from this spot
> till the flowers come

They chop and shred. I'm used to it by now and appreciate it. I think this one too is going down the drain.

We are about to go on to the next person when Charles, who has been silent, says, "Wait. Switch the order and make it two lines. The Japanese love anticipation":

> Awaiting the flowers
> I will not budge

I walk home with a little hop in my step — whether from my haiku or theirs, I do not know.

We get a notice a week later: Next month, try *haibun* if you want.

Haibun is how Basho created his traveling journals. A bit of prose, then a haiku, prose, haiku, prose, haiku.

An hour before our next meeting, I'm sure I shouldn't go. My life has been too busy; I've written nothing. I'm sitting at my desk. I have a half hour to write. *Just try it*, I think. *Be a sport.*

I write about a hike I took one Sunday. Prose, which I'm used to writing, seems to launch me. The words flow.

I walk to Upaya Zen Center, a half block away, to make copies. I arrive at the library a little late. For the first time, only seven people have shown up. Even Charles and Cynthia aren't there.

I can't wait to read mine, unsure where this enthusiasm is coming from.

Alanna reads first:

> dove feathers
> the shadow
> of a hawk

She reads it again.

Someone comments: "Not anything extra. I like it."

Someone else says, "Two images obviously related. It's up to us to figure out how related?"

Another person asks, "Do you need any more feedback?"

She shakes her head.

Two people read their *haibun*. Scott reads one about not wanting children: three short prose sections, each followed by a haiku, exploring condoms, a father's love, a mother's claim.

The next *haibun* is about crossing the border at El Paso at age sixteen to get married. The haiku leaps from the prose to what seems to be a liver transplant many years later.

My curiosity is piqued. I can't help breaking decorum and asking: "Did the marriage last? Is the haiku about the same husband?" It is.

Finally, it's my turn. I read:

Climbing higher than I've ever gone, wanting to see the aspens yellowing earlier than normal, I keep going. Three memorials for friends in September and others sick. A small spring comes down from a higher mountain. Big boulders in shade. A cool spot to meditate.

> Fast mountain creek
> In dark, cold stones
> my original face

A long pause. I cock my head.

"I think it works," says someone.

Someone else says, "Maybe take out 'three memorials.'"

Someone else says, "No, that fits."

I say, "And the haiku?"

Sharon nods. "It's good."

I burst inside, like a firecracker. It's been three decades since I felt like this after finishing a poem. I want to do somersaults, flips, across the room.

Turning

A few days after meeting Harada-san, we are headed for Akame Falls, a series of forty-eight waterfalls in the mountains.

We pick up a map at the park entrance, pay our four hundred yen each, and read how "it was famous for the beauty of nature and also known as a place where ninja, secret agents in feudal times, trained. Fresh air and the sound of falls will make you feel refreshed and relaxed. Enjoy!"

We open the map to sketches of the meandering path and the names of each waterfall along the way. The chilled autumn air is sharp; the foliage bursts with red, subtle yellow, muted brown. Some trees are still green. All of it is reflected in the hard-driving river and in the pools with floating fallen leaves.

Only a few older Japanese couples and a handful of kids are here, mostly at the lower falls. We climb upward without speaking, our ears filled with the splashing sounds of water dropping straight down, sometimes trickling. My favorite falls reminds me of a woman leaning back naked, with her wet hair dipping into the wide pool below.

We stop halfway up to sit on a bench and write for half an hour.

Then we meditate on the same bench, our backs against the moist, cold stone wall, where moss and small ferns live in the cracks and crevices. Random drops of water make the stones look polished in the light filtering through the trees.

We continue to climb up stone steps, hard dirt paths, sometimes a metal stairwell, winding and turning higher and higher. An occasional platform juts out into the river mist, and we get a close-up of a waterfall.

Eventually I lose count of how many waterfalls we've seen. How could there be so many?

Finally we reach the last one, where we sit zazen again on a huge fallen tree trunk overlooking an indigo basin.

We stop for zazen yet again halfway down.

After the final sitting, I say, "You know, even though we followed Basho's path on this trip, it was Buson who brought me here. He said something like this: 'Even though Basho is my great teacher, I don't closely follow his style. I just go by my own will and enjoy the different atmospheres of yesterday and today.'" I push the wool cap off my face. "It's said that Buson was a poet of spring and summer, and Basho was a poet of autumn and winter."

I turn to my two friends. "Do you want to hear Buson's final death poem?"

They don't need to nod. I recite:

> With white plum blossoms
> these nights to the faint light of dawn
> are turning

Alastair turns his head away. He does not want us to see his tears.

Armely says softly, "Say it again."

I repeat it, in a voice just above a whisper:

> With white plum blossoms
> these nights to the faint light of dawn
> are turning

The Sound of Water

Our final stop is Kyoto, a city I admit I don't feel an affinity for. So many electric wires hanging in the air. On some streets they seem to blot out the sky. How many refrigerators, hair dryers, computers, and phones can there be? Yet everyone exclaims Kyoto's beauty.

Ted, an old American acquaintance whom I know from Upaya Zen Center in Santa Fe, picks us up in his car. His five-year-old daughter, Sowa, is with him. He has been in Japan for years, working as a writer and a group travel guide. He has promised to take us to "some place" in the mountains. He does not explain where, but I am happy not to get on a crowded bus, train, or subway for one day. We climb higher and higher, away from the city, and finally park at the side of the road.

We walk down a path and into an open temple complex. Someone is selling incense and plastic bottles of water. I'm walking a little behind the other four. Ted is holding Sowa's hand. She rode in the back seat with us, and I teased her about not sharing her candy. I grabbed for her little hand, clutching a taffy in a fist behind her back. Smart little girl, she dished it right back, lunged for my hand hiding a chocolate.

Soon we are standing before a small, nondescript pond in front of a temple. We gaze down on small goldfish in cloudy water. A single lily pad with no lily floats in the middle. The clipped shrubs around the pond seem dried out.

We stand over the pond with the dazed eyes of tourists, not sure what we are supposed to be looking at. Most ponds in Japan are lively, with koi the size of your legs, swimming and searching for food. I'm used to rippling, clear water over well-placed rocks, wooden bridges, and beaming green plants.

Ted tells us that this temple is old, built during the Heian era, 794–1185. This pond looks old too — or weary.

Then Ted says, matter-of-factly, "This is the pond where Basho wrote his famous haiku."

Time stops. *Of course there had to be a specific pond, a specific moment. That's how a haiku is created.*

We bend down, pick up pebbles. We throw them in.

Plop! Water sound.

We have to hear the sound for ourselves, even though a sign warns us in Japanese, *No stone throwing.*

Ted adds, "Few people — even the Japanese — are aware of this."

We walk back to the car, past a huge yellowing ginkgo tree.

———

Ted then drives us to Basho's grave in Otsu, which is also on the outskirts of Kyoto, in a busy suburb with lots of concrete, paved streets, and curbs. *So this is where he ended?* I think. It's a Sunday. Luckily, there's little traffic so we can park nearby — it's off limits, but we take a chance. We traverse a small parking lot and hurry across an empty street to the temple gates. We enter.

The world suddenly becomes verdant, full of trees and the sound of birds. It is a small, concise temple garden. We pass by the temple office on the right, and Ted points to a stone grave on the left. "Basho."

I fall to my knees, do three full prostrations on that uneven path as a gesture of reverence.

When I'm done, and standing again, Ted says, "Sorry. I made a mistake." He gestures a few yards away. "Here's Basho." He explains that I'd prostrated to the old pond haiku, carved in stone.

I laugh and nod and throw myself in front of the actual person. No person, really. Time wears it all away — past, present. Who is Basho? Where is he now? All those long years since I first read him in my adobe bedroom. How hungry and young I was. Years pour through me as I prostrate, stunned that I am in this moment. So happy to honor him.

Across from the grave is a short footbridge over another pond. Sowa counts eight snapping turtles hiding in the rocks.

A persimmon tree, gold and heavy with ripe fruit, stands at the far end of the courtyard. I see Armely spying a persimmon that hangs low, in reach. She starts to walk toward it, then stops. One can't steal from the temple grounds.

Sowa announces to her father that she is hungry. I am too and oddly ready to leave.

Ted asks, "Is it okay to go to a Western chain?" He angles his head down, indicating his daughter. "It's just easier."

"Sure," I say. Actually, I'm delighted. I'm more than ready for the food I grew up with.

Sowa, across from me, orders noodles. I order steak with fries and an endless tap of Coke. I shove my empty glass into the bin of cracked ice, then under the spigot with the red-and-white sign.

By the time our meal is served, I've already bloated myself with two glasses.

On the third saunter to the machine I hear out of no-where Katagiri Roshi's voice reciting Basho:

> Matsushima ah
> Matsushima ah
> ah, Matsushima

This haiku is at least three hundred fifty years old. Roshi recited it one evening during one of his regular Wednesday-night lectures in Minneapolis, that flat American city near the edge of the Great Plains, the wind drifting snow across the frozen surface of Lake Calhoun.

For forty years, since I first heard him recite this haiku, I thought Matsushima was a mountain. I wanted to see for myself what made it so special, so enthralling, the source of so many sighs. So, on this trip, Matsushima was the first place I insisted we go after we arrived in Tokyo. To my surprise, it's not a mountain at all but a cluster of open islands off the coast of Honshu. When Basho reached them after his long trek, he was speechless at their beauty.

I was excited, agitated, when we arrived: Would I see what he saw? I paused and had a big gulp of water, *yes*, standing on shore looking out, *yes, they were radiant*. The whole scene was astounding. Basho's haiku fell deeper inside me.

Basho never wrote this haiku down, and for more than a century, perhaps longer, this haiku remained part of an oral tradition, handed down from generation to generation. And at this point people are not even sure Basho uttered it. Does it even matter? Maybe that was the point Roshi was trying to make — about the lineage, the echo of emptiness passed on, only through breath's evanescence.

Later, I find out that in Basho's time, Japanese poets were largely imitating Chinese culture, and much of the poetry was still written at least partly in Chinese. It would be very Chinese to note the croaking of the frog in a haiku about an old pond. But what Basho called out instead was the sound of the water. This was purely Japanese, purely original.

Perhaps that's why this haiku is so revered. It broke a tradition, a paradigm, a way of seeing. The Japanese became more of who they were, standing in their own worldview. What a splash that was, what a frog, what a pond. It has shimmered through the centuries — not only the water, but the mind transmitting it, in three simple, direct lines called haiku.

Epilogue: Another World

In Mill Valley, California, in 1997, I was subletting a friend's apartment, struggling to finish a difficult manuscript. For four days in a row I could not sleep. I tossed and turned until dawn, not knowing what was wrong. Each day I felt more lost, more despairing.

On the fourth day of no sleep, in early afternoon, I wandered up and down the streets of this small, fashionable hill town. In the distance was Mount Tamalpais, considered sacred to the Coast Miwok people.

My shoulders were tight. I had a tic in my left eye. My thumb and index finger felt raw from so little rest, on top of struggling with my writing.

I stopped walking and sat at the bottom of a long flight of stairs leading to a stranger's front door. I leaned back and stared up at the tossing of Monterey pine boughs high above. In my broken, tired state I was actually able to see the wind, the frenzy of air, moving the pines. I began sobbing. My chest heaved wildly, as though my heart would break out of its cage. My eyes flooded with tears. Yet I did not know what or who I was grieving.

After a while, drained, I lifted myself off the step and me-
andered down the house-lined streets. I went into a little lun-
cheonette and ordered a hamburger and fries. While I waited
for my food, I picked up a local newspaper left on the table.

I read the headline: "Allen Ginsberg, Beat Generation
Poet, Author of the Famous Poem *Howl*, Is Dead."

Allen had been ailing from hepatitis and congestive heart
failure. Ann Waldman, a poet and close friend of Allen's, told
me months before when we were teaching in the same place
in New York that she had visited Allen in the hospital. It was
right after the doctor had diagnosed liver cancer and told him
he didn't have long to live. She said they clung to each other
and wept. Then she left and when she hit the street, she turned
around and went back into the building. She couldn't leave
him like that. She took the elevator and when she came to his
doorway he was no longer crying. Leaning over his notebook,
he was working on a poem. She quietly walked away.

Surrounded by friends and old lovers in his East Village
loft, he passed away on April 5, 1997. Yesterday.

He stayed up his entire final night, calling friends to say
goodbye and asking if they needed money. He'd gotten rich
selling all his papers to a university.

That was Allen, the bighearted, generous man I knew.

The waitress came with my order. I ate two fries, left everything else on the plate, fumbled for my wallet, paid the bill,
and walked out the door.

Allen was the man who introduced me to the study of
mind and connected it to writing. This alone opened my
world, illuminated my vision of being a writer, and gave me

my life's path and practice. I have stayed true to it ever since. Ten years after I took his class I wrote *Writing Down the Bones*. Later I had the privilege of teaching with him in Los Angeles, but I don't think I ever properly communicated how influential he was to me. I was still shy and in awe.

When my difficult manuscript was finished and eventually published, I dedicated it to him.

But only now, more than two decades later, when I am the age he was when he died, do I realize that those four nights of sleeplessness, and those wild minutes of full-throated grief, were all about his final illness and death — that wind I saw overhead — the Tibetans say it's the spirit leaving.

Allen, I wrote these for you:

> Allen Ginsberg
> far beyond
> seventeen syllables
>
> Spring wind
> blossomed you
> into another world

Haiku Lesson

Probably two decades ago I taught a year-long intensive, in which each student had to choose a practice for the full year. Beth Howard from Wyoming chose writing a haiku a day. When the year was up she continued.

I said to her at some point, "Tell me what you have discovered the rules to be."

I have a card from her that she sent in 2015 listing them. Recently I called her and she said, "Oh, let me see them. They would probably be all different now."

"No," I retorted. "I want to keep your first thoughts."

So here they are.

1. The first thing is to *let go*. To really enter what is before you, around you, there is a lot you have to let go of. It doesn't help to *look* for a haiku, but it does help to be clear — a blank slate — so a haiku can write itself in you.

2. Use an unfocused gaze or a wider view and perception. Our mind interferes with what we see and hear — often choosing to notice the familiar. In any

given instant there are so many things we do not see or hear or feel. It reminds me of the unfocused gaze we use in sitting meditation. As if using peripheral vision/hearing, etc. to see/hear whatever else is there.

3. Notice the connections…to a person or a feeling if it's there. This is the leap that happens in haiku when a connection is there. This also is not something to look for or aim for, it doesn't work — just let go — open to *all* that is in the moment.

4. Write it down. I thought I would remember. I never remember (or hardly ever). Small memo pads are all you need, nothing fancy.

5. Put down every line that comes — there may be more than one choice that sounds right. Put them all down in the moment. You don't have to finish the haiku in the moment, but you don't want to lose it.

6. *Revise.* Make it crystal clear. Remove anything not needed. Did you use the best word to catch the moment? Do you feel the moment when you read it? Is something missing?

> one cold day to another
> linked like a freight train
> cannot see the end

> forget-me-nots
> beside pathway to lakeshore
> missing my parents

leaves show each day
effortlessly
how to let go

winter evening
great horned owl calls
one brief life

diving face-first
into lavender blossom
bumblebee

almost forgetting
tiny maple leaves open
son is at war

hickory
strange nut
like me

to learn how to live
watch the full moon rise

BETH HOWARD

Acknowledgments

First and foremost I'd like to thank Alastair Smith and Armely Matas for accompanying me on the 2016 Basho trek in Japan. My heartfelt gratitude.

Thank you also to Deb and Bob Merion, who lent me their condo in Florida to write the first fifty pages in a flurry before I went home to cancer treatment. Gratitude to the Bloedel Reserve on Bainbridge Island, Washington; the Ucross Foundation, in Clearmont, Wyoming; the Centrum Artist Residency, in Port Townsend, Washington; the Mabel Dodge Luhan House in Taos, New Mexico — all for providing me space over the past three years to work on this book.

Also much gratitude to Eddie Lewis, John Dear, Susana Guillaume, Baksim Goddard, Joanne Hunt, Wendy Johnson, Armely Matas, Bill Addison, and Pearlie Loo for their initial reads of the manuscript at different levels of completion.

Thank you to Clark Strand, who many years ago introduced me to Shiki. Thanks to Joan Halifax and Kaz Tanahashi for teaching haiku weekends with me at Upaya Zen Center for the past six years and to Clark Strand for joining us in the last three. Also thanks to Kaz, who helped translate a haiku by Fumiko Harada many, many months after it was written.

A long gratitude to Clara Rosemarda, who has sustained me with good advice for more than thirty years.

Thank you to St. John's College bookstore, where I have discovered so many great haiku books and translations.

Appreciation to Saundra Goldman, who found for me the first biography I read of Basho.

Thank you to Branwyn Pinkerton, who diligently typed this manuscript, not once, but over and over as I edited. Gratitude to Dorotea Mendoza, who pinched-hit typing when I was in her hometown of Brooklyn.

So many people supported me directly or indirectly in the creation of this book, knowingly or not — Jacqueline West, Laura Counsel, Martha Worthley, Sharon Dynak, Julie Keefe, Jennifer Brown, Tracey Kikut, Beth Howard, Will Hewett, Genzan Quennell, Renee Gregorio, John Brandi, Alice Shorett, Dave Shorett, and everyone in the monthly Haiku Study Group.

Special hats off to Scott Edelstein, who helped with the basic structure of the book and also actively and with awareness placed the book in its rightful home.

Thank you, Jason Gardner, my editor; I'd been waiting at least three years to have the opportunity for us to work together.

And thank you to everyone who is not named here. You are not forgotten.

And if you are interested in venturing to Japan (or Germany), Mitsue Nagase, who is featured in this book, is a photographer based in Kyoto and Berlin. She, along with her partner, Bernd Schellhorn, organizes and guides wonderful custom-tailored tours and study trips for small groups. Please visit www.schellhorn-nagase.com.

Permissions

Basho, "A cold rain starting," "Don't imitate me," and "The summer grass" from Robert Hass, *The Essential Haiku*. Copyright © 1994 by Robert Hass. Reprinted by permission of Harper-Collins Publishers and Bloodaxe Books, Ltd.

Alanna C. Burke, "Dove feathers" from *Creatrix* 42 (September 2018). Reprinted by permission of the author.

Buson, "The piercing cold —" from Patricia Donegan, *Haiku Mind*. Copyright © 2009 by Patricia Donegan. Reprinted by permission of the Permissions Company, LLC, on behalf of Shambhala Publications, Inc., Boulder, Colorado, shambhala.com. "Ah, grief and sadness!" from R. H. Blyth, *Haiku*. Copyright © 1981 by R. H. Blyth. "In the summer rain," "The two plum trees —," and "I go," from Robert Hass, *The Essential Haiku*. Copyright © 1994 by Robert Hass. Reprinted by permission of Harper-Collins Publishers and Bloodaxe Books, Ltd. "The rainy season," "The high priest," "I grasp," "A bad-tempered priest," "An evening shower!," "They look beautiful," "Morning glories —," "River in winter —," "Camphor tree roots," "Going off to sleep," "While feeling sad —," "For the Death Anniversary of Basho," "Following the Master's Poem," "No trail to follow," "A winter night!" and "With white plum blossoms" from *Haiku*

Sources and Recommended Reading

Sources

Aitken, Robert. *Zen Wave: Basho's Haiku and Zen*. New York: Weatherhill, 1978.

Basho, Matsuo. *Basho and His Interpreters: Selected Hokku with Commentary*. Edited and translated by Makoto Ueda. Redwood City, CA: Stanford University Press, 1992.

———. *Narrow Road to the Interior: And Other Writings*. Translated by Sam Hamill. Boulder, CO: Shambhala, 1998.

———. *Basho's Haiku: Selected Poems of Matsuo Basho*. Translated by David Landis Barnhill. Albany, NY: State University of New York Press, 2004.

Beichman, Janine. *Masaoka Shiki: His Life and Works*. Boston: Cheng & Tsui, 2002.

Blyth, R.H., ed. *Haiku, Volume 1: Eastern Culture*. Tokyo: Hokuseido, 1949.

———. *Haiku, Volume 2: Spring*. Tokyo: Hokuseido, 1950.

———: *Haiku, Volume 3: Summer–Autumn*. Tokyo: Hokuseido, 1952.

———. *Haiku, Volume 4: Autumn–Winter*. Tokyo: Hokuseido, 1952.

Buson, Yosa. *Haiku Master Buson*. Translated by Yuki Sawa and
 Edith Marcombe Shiffert. Buffalo, NY: White Pine Press, 2007.

Donegan, Patricia. *Haiku Mind: 108 Poems to Cultivate Awareness
 and Open Your Heart*. Boulder, CO: Shambhala, 2008.

Donegan, Patricia, and Yoshie Ishibashi. *Chiyo-ni: Woman Haiku
 Master*. North Clarendon, VT: Tuttle, 1998.

French, Calvin L. *The Poet-Painters: Buson and His Followers*. Ann
 Arbor, MI: University of Michigan Museum of Art, 1974.

Hamill, Sam, trans. *The Pocket Haiku*. Boulder, CO: Shambhala,
 2014.

Hass, Robert, ed. and trans. *The Essential Haiku: Versions of Basho,
 Buson, & Issa*. New York: Ecco, 1995.

Hoffmann, Yoel, ed. *Japanese Death Poems: Written by Zen Monks
 and Haiku Poets on the Verge of Death*. Clarendon, VT: Tuttle,
 1986.

Issa, Kobayashi. *The Year of My Life: A Translation of Issa's Oraga
 Haru*. Translated by Nobuyuki Yuasa. Berkeley: University of
 California Press, 1960.

———. *Inch by Inch: 45 Haiku by Issa*. Translated by Nanao
 Sakaki. Corrales, NM: Tooth of Time Books, 1985.

———. *Issa's Best: A Translator's Selection of Master Haiku*.
 Translated by David G. Lanoue. HaikuGuy.com, 2012.

Kakuzo, Okakura. *The Book of Tea*. New York: Duffield, 1906.

Keene, Donald. *The Winter Sun Shines In: A Life of Masaoka Shiki*.
 New York: Columbia University Press, 2013.

Kern, Adam, trans. *The Penguin Book of Haiku*. New York: Penguin,
 2018.

Shiki, Masaoka. *Masaoka Shiki: Selected Poems*. Translated by
 Burton Watson. New York: Columbia University Press, 1997.

———. *A House by Itself: Selected Haiku of Shiki*. Translated by
 John Brandi and Noriko Kawasaki Martinez. Buffalo, NY:
 White Pine Press, 2017.

Ueda, Makoto. *The Master Haiku Poet Matsuo Basho*. Tokyo:
    Kodansha, 1982.

Books on Haiku in General

These books helped to inform my understanding of haiku, its development, and its possible scope and were read before or intermittently as I worked on this book.

Kacian, Jim, Philip Rowland, and Allan Burns, eds. *Haiku in
    English: The First Hundred Years*. New York: Norton, 2016.
Koren, Leonard. *Wabi-Sabi for Artists, Designers, Poets & Philoso-
    phers*. Point Reyes, CA: Imperfect Publishing, 1994.
Strand, Clark. *Seeds from a Birch Tree: Writing Haiku and the
    Spiritual Journey*. New York: Hyperion, 1998.
Suzuki, Mitsu. *A White Tea Bowl: 100 Haiku from 100 Years of Life*.
    Translated by Kate Mccandless. Berkeley, CA: Rodmell, 2008.
Trumbull, Charles. *A History of Modern Haiku*. Lincoln, IL: Mod-
    ern Haiku Press, 2019.
Ueda, Makoto, ed. and trans. *Far Beyond the Field: Haiku by Japa-
    nese Women*. New York: Columbia University Press, 2003.
Wright, Richard. *Haiku: The Last Poems of an American Icon*. New
    York: Anchor, 1998.

About the Author

Natalie Goldberg is the author of fifteen books, including *Writing Down the Bones*, which has changed the way writing is taught in the United States. She has also written the beloved memoir *Long Quiet Highway*; the novel *Banana Rose*; *Living Color*, about her painting; and her legacy book, *The True Secret of Writing*.

She has taught writing as a practice for the past forty-five years nationally and internationally. She lives in northern New Mexico. For more information, please visit www.natalie goldberg.com.